CHASING
AMERICAN
LEGENDS
The Workbook

COPYRIGHT

Additional materials available from:

Patriot Academy
P.O. Box 586
Dripping Springs, TX 78620
512-515-3744
PatriotAcademy.com

Design:

Joshua Russell

ISBN 978-0-9981269-0-6

Printed in the United States of America

TABLE OF CONTENTS

Bulletproof President?

It was more than a battle. More than a story from the history books.

With its awe-inspiring example of courage and trust, the Battle of the Monongahela's invigorating illustration of God's power in the life of Washington immediately captured my admiration. I had never heard of this battle until a few days before my family visited Braddock's Field, Penn.

But as soon as I did, I was super excited to bust out the historic books from The Vault with the rest of the family. We learned amazing truths about Washington, his perseverance, and his courage. Because some were a bit skeptical (UNCLE BRAD!!!), we eagerly decided to test a few theories after actually visiting the spot where the battle took place.

We gathered Trey and Rhett's homemade and awesome, I might add, paintball guns, and made some measurements in order to replicate the scene as accurately as we could. (We were a few Indians short, but we figured six of us would have to do)

Loading up our guns, we opened fire, pelting poor Uncle Brad with colors of pink and blue.

Our test proved that it shouldn't have been possible for Washington to stay alive, seeing how badly Uncle Brad's limp was after being shot with just balls of paint, instead of real musket balls :)

There were only six of us. Six! More than 100x that, over 600 men, were trying to paint Washington with red (and that doesn't include the French). Only by the great hand of God did he make it through the gunfire and the smoke, the screams, and the death.

I'm more than grateful that my family had the opportunity to see and study where Washington made a critical mark in history on that summer day in 1755.

It's one I'll never forget.

- Kamryn

The Facts:

George Washington survived the Battle of Monongahela with four musket ball holes through his coat, two horses shot out from under him, and his tricorn hat shot from off his head. Out of the 80 officers that went into the battle, 63 were either killed or wounded, yet Washington survived the battle unscathed.

The Myth:

Was Washington protected by the powerful hand of Divine Providence? Or, were the French simply horrible at aiming and Washington insanely lucky?

EPISODE 1

The investigation for this episode began with a visit from our good friend, comedian Brad Stine. Brad had been searching for some

good stories to include in our Legends of Liberty book series and could not believe the story of George Washington's heroic and miraculous survival at the Battle of the Monongahela (see if you can pronounce that any better than Brad!).

French and Indian War (1756-1763)

The French and Indian War was a series of military engagements between two coalition armies, one led by France and the other by Great Britain. It was actually a small part of a larger war that was occurring worldwide between many European nations, called the "Seven Years War." In North America, the armies of both Great Britain and France were comprised of trained regulars, local militias, and local Indian tribes who chose sides in the fight.

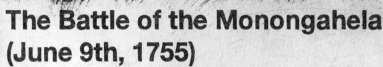

The Battle of the Monongahela (June 9th, 1755)

The Battle of the Monongahela, the turning point in young Colonel George Washington's military career, was a major defeat for the British forces during the war. It occurred during the "Braddock Expedition," led by esteemed British General Edward Braddock. Attempting to capture Fort Duquesne, the British were ambushed by French troops within just 10 miles of the Fort. Being unfamiliar with the guerilla fighting style of the Indian tribes, who made up the majority of the French forces, the British forces were very quickly cut to ribbons by the concentrated fire on their position, which was a narrow road snaking its way through the forest.

Although he was said to have fought bravely, the leader of the British forces, General Braddock, fell wounded early in the battle and would die just days later. Colonel George Washington, although having no official place in the command structure (he was simply there to help guide and advise General Braddock), took command of the forward part of the army and successfully lead them

in a retreat back to their reserve force. He did this by riding up and down the British line on horseback, making himself an easy target for the French and Indian snipers, yet also inspiring the British troops and showing them that he did not fear their enemy. Even though Washington had multiple examples of near mortal wounds: such as having two horses shot out from under him, his hat shot off of his head, and four musket ball holes through his coat, he left the battle completely unscathed.

Although they later recovered, the defeat at Monongahela ended the "Braddock Expedition," an attempt at a major incursion into French territory. Yet, out of that defeat came some measure of victory, as the battle gave young Washington the chance to show his true colors and ability as a leader by saving the British army.

Some help from The Vault

As we began our research, we received an amazing treasure trove of original documents from our friends at The Vault (see Episode 5 for more about The Vault).

THE VAULT / Is home to over 100,000 documents and artifacts

8

What did eye witnesses say about Washington during the Battle of the Monongahela?

When investigating the myth of "Bulletproof George Washington," some of the best sources are the eye-witness accounts of the individuals who were at the battle that day. One of which, is Washington himself! In a letter to his brother, John Augustine Washington, He said...

> "But by the All-powerful Dispensations of Providence, I have been protected beyond all human probability or expectation, for I had four Bullets through my Coat and two Horses shot out Under me; yet escaped unhurt, although Death was leveling my Companions on every side of me!"

So...Washington most definitely believed that Providence played a part in protecting him through the battle.

What about the enemy? What did they believe happened? Were they possibly just untrained? Did the smoke from the muskets create a fog so thick they just couldn't see Washington? Neither of those would make sense or be consistent with the facts, since it is clear that the French forces quite easily fought off the British and took down almost every other single British officer other than Washington.

So what made Washington different?

There are multiple accounts from the Indian forces that shed light on their opinion of what happened that day. Red Hawk, an important Indian chief integral to the French's victory at  Monongahela, was well known for never missing a shot. He said he shot eleven different times at Washington that day without hitting him. Because he had never missed in battle before, Red Hawk stopped shooting, convinced that Washington was protected by the "Great Spirit."

Another famous Indian sniper and leader in the ambush on the British forces was often heard testifying about his inability to hit Washington. He said...

"Washington was never born to be killed by a bullet! I had seventeen fair fires at him with my rifle, and after all could not bring him to the ground!"

Fifteen years after the Battle of the Monongahela, Washington and his friend Dr. James Craik were traveling towards the western territories of North America to explore uninhabited regions. While camped, a group of Indians led by an older war chief approached Washington's camp and requested to speak with him. Using an interpreter, that war chief spoke to Washington about the Battle of the Monongahela, where they were both present. Here is what he said to Washington...

"It was on the day when the white man's blood mixed with the streams of our forest that I first beheld this chief [indicating Washington]. I called to my young men and said, "Mark yon tall and daring warrior? He is not of the red-coat tribe – he hath an Indian's wisdom, and his warriors fight as we do – himself is alone exposed. Quick! Let your aim be certain, and he dies." Our rifles were leveled – rifles which, but for you, knew not how to miss. 'Twas all in vain; a power mightier far than we shielded you. Seeing you were under the special guardian-ship of the Great Spirit, we immediately ceased to fire at you. I am old, and soon shall be gathered to the great council fire of my fathers in the land of shades; but ere I go, there is something bids me speak in the voice of prophecy. Listen! The Great Spirit protects that man [again indicating Washington], and guides his destinies- he will become the chief of nations, and a people yet unborn will hail him as the founder of a mighty empire. I am come to pay homage to the man who is the particular favorite of Heaven and who can never die in battle."

After reading the words of the Indians, it is difficult to doubt their sincerity in believing that Washington was protected by an outside force. Moreover, Washington himself couldn't believe that he made it out of the battle  by any other reason than the hand of God. Were they both correct? Or is there a chance that Washington was simply lucky?

The more that we began to research the battle, the more that I became convinced that God had his hand on Washington. After walking the actual road where Washington stood more than 260 years ago... and seeing just how close the French and Indian troops were to the British, I couldn't find a logical explanation for how Washington possibly survived the slaughter that occurred there. The only viable answer was that Providence was at play. My brothers and Brad were still very skeptical though. Despite the overwhelming evidence, they still believed there was a chance that someone could be lucky and escape unharmed from the battle. For them, one final test remained... recreating the battle scene! After taking pictures and measurements of Braddock's road, we made our way back to Texas to replicate the environment of the battle as best we could, in our own fun way! The first positive thing about our test was that unlike Pennsylvania in December, Texas wasn't snowing! It never snows where we live... sad, I know, but the lack of snow actually made the scene more realistic, since the real battle took place in the heat of June. We measured off the same width as Braddock's road had been in the battle, and got Brad a couple of "horses" to ride. Trey made everyone in the family a modified paintball gun that fired similar to muskets back in the 1700s. My brothers fired

a few test shots and didn't do very well... I fired three shots and hit the target twice! Girl power! Ha! Take that boys. We

got in position and Uncle Brad came out obviously enjoying his part as George Washington. We were ready to go!

EPISODE 1

What I Learned:

I learned quite a few things while investigating the story of George Washington. After finishing our test with Brad, I was completely convinced that there is no reason, other than supernatural protection, that Washington  should have survived the Battle of the Monongahela. My brothers were even finally convinced after they saw how easy it was to hit Brad with our musket style paintball guns! The only viable answer was that God had something special in mind for Washington and protected him through the battle because of it. I'd say that this myth is proven to be correct, at least as correct as we'll ever know. Something was protecting Washington during the Battle of the Monongahela, and I think the facts prove that something was the Hand of Divine Providence.

– Kamryn Green

P.S. Here are a couple of things that I took away from this investigation!

1. God uses His Providence as a way of helping to guide mankind. God knew that America would need George Washington to lead us through our early years. If God had not protected Washington, where would our nation be today? There's a good chance America might not even exist. Through all the chaos and fighting that surrounded the creation of our

great nation, Washington was a steady hand and guiding voice to the American people.

2. Myths can be easily investigated when you do the right research! It was so funny to see how easily the question was originally answered when we began looking at the eye witness accounts who saw Washington that day. Whenever someone makes a claim about history, or tries to debunk a myth, ask them if they have ever looked at original sources. Those sources will usually have the correct answers!

EPISODE 1

Discussion Questions

1. What was the name of the battle where George Washington was rumored to be "Bulletproof?"

2. Who were the British fighting against during the attempted expedition?

3. What was the name of the British General who was wounded in the ambush, thereby shifting the mantle of leadership during the battle to Washington?

4. How many British officers, out of the original 80, were either killed or wounded during the battle?

5. What was the name of the Indian sniper who had never missed a shot in battle before attempting to shoot at Washington and who believed that Washington was protected by "The Great Spirit?"

Essay Question

In your own opinion, was Washington protected by Divine Providence or was he just lucky? In either case, state how you came to the conclusion and list the evidence to support it.

Guest Profile:
Brad Stine

The Greens refer to him as 'Uncle Brad', but Brad Stine is an award winning comic and pundit with an impressive theatrical career as well. He can make the most inane topics side-splittingly funny, but  he has a commanding knowledge of practically everything. Recently Brad is on a personal journey to rediscover America's lost legacies, and he will often times invite himself along on the Green family's journeys to get a firsthand look at the past. But Brad has a twisted tendency to get into trouble, and is constantly getting into hijinks.

Special Mention:
Braddock's Battlefield History Center

Braddock's Battlefield History Center opened in August of 2012. It commemorates one of the most famous military engagements in the history of Colonial America, the Battle of the Monongahela. The founder and curator is Mr.

ROBERT T. MESSNER
MUSEUM FOUNDER, CURATOR

Robert T. Messner, who was a wealth of information and excellent tour guide for the Green Family when it came to learning more about Washington and the famous battle. The Greens are very thankful for the work of Mr. Messner, who is preserving history for people like us to come and learn! Please visit the Center's website at
http://www.braddocksbattlefield.com/

Lives, Fortunes, and Sacred Honor

There are few places I enjoy visiting as much as Independence Hall, in the heart of Philadelphia. I always make sure to take the kids to the Museum of Art, so that we can run up those 72 stone steps just like Rocky Balboa! There is so much history in Philadelphia that you can almost feel the presence of greatness surrounding the heart of the city. We were blessed to be in Philadelphia for this episode to speak to a group of business leaders, in the actual Independence Hall where the Founding Fathers stood and built our great nation. Tracing their footsteps, standing where they hammered out our founding documents, you get chills…you can still feel the courage of their convictions.

Unfortunately for us on this particular trip, the federal government decided to experience a funding crisis right as we flew into Philadelphia! What are the odds of that? While it caused some scrambling on our end, it made for an interesting episode, and ended up working out after all. Not only did the kids get the chance to see some cool places while looking for a back-up venue, but we ultimately still had the privilege of speak in my favorite historical site, Independence Hall. It was an honor for the Green family to teach and share the stories of this hallowed ground of history. This was a very special trip that we will never forget.

- Rick

The Challenge:

Find a new venue as historic as Independence Park before our guests arrive for the Constitution Class we're teaching. (while praying the government shutdown ends and the Park Rangers can open in time!)

THE GREEN FAMILY TRAVELS AND SPEAKS AROUND THE NATION TO AUDIENCES AS LARGE AS 15,000

EPISODE 2

EPISODE 2

With less than 10 hours to find a backup venue, we decided to split up in our search. The extra benefit was that everyone had the chance to visit some cool sights we would not have seen in our regular schedule. You'll see them in the episode, but we've included some additional fun facts and information here for study! - Rick

Christ Church in Philadelphia

Trey and Reagan were convinced they found the perfect location on their very first stop. Also known as "The Nation's Church," because of how many founding fathers and other revolutionary era leaders worshiped there, Christ Church is filled with history and charm. Founded in 1695, Christ Church is actually the birthplace of the

Benjamin Franklin, Joseph Hewes, Francis Hopkinson, Robert Morris, George Ross, Dr Benjamin Rush, and James Wilson are all buried at Christ Church. Seven Signers!

American Episcopal Church. It was known for becoming the home church for many members of the Continental Congress, as well as Presidents Washington and Adams.

Baptizing both free and enslaved blacks, and opening her doors to all who wished to attend services and enjoy the word of God, Christ Church quickly became a beacon of hope for the community. Many historical figures, including seven signers of the Declaration of Independence, are buried on Christ Church property. There are also many military figures, explorers, and various revolutionary-era leaders buried alongside the signers.

The Graff House

THE DECLARATION HOUSE

aka 'The Graff House', where Thomas Jefferson lived in 1776 while he wrote the Declaration of Independence. Built in 1775, rebuilt in 1975 by the National Park Service.

While Trey and Reagan were at Christ Church, the rest of the family was trying to get in to see the Graff House. Also known as The Declaration House, this is where Thomas Jefferson lived while he wrote the Declaration of Independence in 1776. Named after its owner Jacob Graff, Jefferson lived in the rooms on the second floor while penning one of the greatest achievements and documents of any human writer in history. Sadly, in the late 1800s, the original house owned by Jacob Graff was deconstructed to make way for city expansion, destroying a priceless piece of history. The house was reconstructed in 1975 using accurate architectural plans of the original home and many authentic furnishings.

Independence Hall

Much to our relief, the Park Rangers came through like champs and were able to open Independence Park just in time for our class. Originally constructed in 1732 for the purpose

of housing Pennsylvania's government, this beautiful building quickly became an important location for the United States. It was loaned out by the Pennsylvania government for the meetings of the Second Continental Congress and later, the Constitutional Convention. It was here in 1775

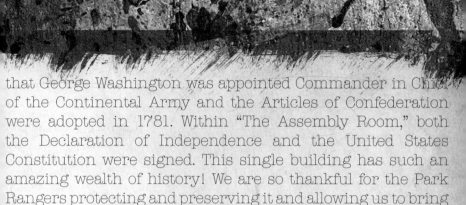

that George Washington was appointed Commander in Chief of the Continental Army and the Articles of Confederation were adopted in 1781. Within "The Assembly Room," both the Declaration of Independence and the United States Constitution were signed. This single building has such an amazing wealth of history! We are so thankful for the Park Rangers protecting and preserving it and allowing us to bring history to life in this very special place.

Congress Hall

Right next to Independence Hall resides Congress Hall, which was the primary place of meeting for our U.S. Congress between 1790-1800. The House of Representatives met on the main floor, while the Senate met upstairs, directly above the house. In addition to housing our legislature, this is the very room where President Washington held his second inauguration, and four years later, the inauguration of President John Adams. This building was home to many landmark actions by the government, including the establishment of the Federal Mint and the creation of the Department of Navy.

EPISODE 2

The Signing of the Declaration!

We believe in the power of re-creating historical moments and replicating the actions of our forefathers. So when we brought out the Declaration and gave everyone the chance to sign it, in Congress Hall itself, you could feel the emotional significance of the moment reverberating throughout the room! It was incredible to see everyone's faces as they comprehended the gravity and seriousness of the moment. Yet, there was joy there also, as each individual came forward and signed the same pledge as the original 56 signers. That pledge states "for the support of this Declaration, with a firm reliance on the protection of Divine Providence, we mutually pledge to each other our Lives, our Fortunes and our Sacred Honor." If you had to give that pledge today, what would it mean to you?

-Rick

The Sacrifice of the Founding Fathers: Lives, Fortunes, and Sacred Honor

It can be difficult for us to imagine what it truly means to pledge everything that we have to a cause. We pledge ourselves to the United States, but our lives are so comfortable in today's society that we struggle to truly understood what the Founding Fathers went through when they made their great pledge. When they signed that document, they quite literally were saying they believed so strongly in freedom, they were willing to completely give up their Lives, Fortunes, and Sacred Honor. For them, that actually meant giving up the things they pledged. Many of them lost their lives to war or prison, many lost their entire fortunes, giving it all to the cause of freedom. Many were hunted and scorned simply for being willing to speak out for freedom. They gave it all to birth this great nation.

Is it too much to ask that each of us be willing to give up only a little to preserve it.

EPISODE 2

The Charge!

This turned out to be a truly inspiring trip for the Green Family. We are so thankful for the opportunity to remind our fellow Americans of the great Blessings we have in this Nation.

Our Founding Fathers pledged their Lives, Fortunes, and Sacred Honor to each other and to the cause of freedom. What is being asked of us today is that we honor their sacrifice by exercising our freedoms and ensuring they are preserved for future generations of Americans. Today, giving of our lives, fortunes, and sacred honor is more of a privilege than a sacrifice. Our Family is asking you to join us in pledging to these three areas below as a way of contributing to the guardianship of freedom.

Lives: Be willing to give just a little bit of time to vote, pray, and carry out our civic responsibilities. Thirty minutes on the weekend to research candidates, or a visit with your local state

representative can go a long way towards determining your vote in future elections, and therefore your influence on our government.

Fortunes: I know it is sometimes hard at first, but have you ever noticed how easy it is to give to a good cause once you see the positive results, the return on investment? Think of the return on investing in the future of liberty! If we desire to protect freedom, if we desire for our kids and grandkids to grow up with the same freedoms we have enjoyed, then we must be willing to give a small portion of our finances to effective organizations and candidates that will defend the principles and strategies of freedom here in America. Unlike the Founding Fathers, we don't have to give every penny we have! We do need to be willing to sacrifice in small ways though. Maybe avoid spending money on Netflix or movies for just a couple of months, and instead send that money to a program that is training up the next generation of leaders. Invest in freedom's future and the payoff will be worth it. Check out PatriotAcademy.com and WallBuilders.com if you'd like to see your 'investments in freedom' bring a great return of liberty for future generations.

Sacred Honor: This might be the toughest sacrifice to make, even above finances. The Founding Fathers were willing to stand against a nation, to stand against a superpower in the name of freedom. Are we willing to stand for those same timeless principles of liberty, even in the free society that we live in today? All it takes for evil to triumph is for good people to do nothing. Evil too often wins today because we are not willing to stand up and fight, even when we are in the majority! We must be willing to speak out, to send a letter to our local newspaper editor or post online, voice support for local candidates, and convince our pastors to begin preaching Biblical principles applied to the world (just like the Black Robe Regiment of the Revolutionary War). More than anything, we must not be afraid to take the step of using the voice and influence God gave each of us. The insults that will be hurled at us for standing for truth are nothing compared to the bullets taken by those who came before us.

The Torch of Freedom is not a self-sustaining flame; it must be guarded, and it must be instilled in each generation. We best honor those who protected our freedom in the past by doing our part today. Live out and fight for your freedom so that it may be passed in tact to the next generation.

– Rick Green

Discussion Questions

1. What is the name of the building where the Declaration and Constitution were signed?
2. Which important document did Thomas Jefferson author while staying at Jacob Graff's house?
3. Which one of George Washington's inaugurations occurred in Congress Hall?
4. Can you name 3 locations the Green's investigated as possible backup venues?

Essay Question

What does it mean to you to give your life, fortune, and sacred honor towards the protection of America and its founding principles?

EPISODE 2

Guest Profile:
Gary Newell

Gary Newell is a former professional football player. After football, he was called to youth ministry and founded Outreach America (for more information visit OutreachAmerica. org). Gary has spoken to over a million young people on four continents and ministers across the globe at camps, conferences, and churches. He is also a successful business owner passionate about sharing lessons on integrity, teamwork, and unity. Gary is a good friend to the Green Family who shares our passion for truth both within today's society and history itself.

Special Mention:
The National Park Service Rangers

The National Park Rangers are in a nutshell, the custodians of our precious historical sites! Park ranger is a broad term for a career that is incredibly multi-faceted and diverse. Park rangers are responsible for protecting our state and national parks. Park rangers may serve as law enforcement officers, nature experts, historians or a combination of the three. The Greens have had the honor of working repeatedly with the Rangers who protect both Independence and Congress Hall. We are eternally grateful for their constant and joyful vigilance in the guardianship of our nation's treasures.

Communist King
or
Peaceful Crusader?

During a performance in Georgia, Dad gave several powerful quotes from Rev. Martin Luther King, Jr. which led to a question from someone claiming that MLK was a communist. Dad wanted to get some first hand facts before launching a defense of one of his heroes, so we began a journey that allowed us to spend time with Rev. King's niece, Dr. Alveda King, in the very church where he preached his first sermon. We also visited the Birmingham Civil Rights Museum and left with a much deeper appreciation for our liberty and the Declaration of Independence principles. Here are a few of the highlights, as well as how it affected our conclusion on Rev. King.

- Kamryn

The Facts:

The Rev. Martin Luther King Jr taught that we are all mankind, and that no one should judge each other based on anything other than their actions. Mutual respect, love for one another, and justice are imperative to human existence.

The Myth:

Did Martin Luther King Jr adapt his principles and philosophy from communist and socialist ideology?

EPISODE 3

Ebenezer Baptist Church

Ebenezer Baptist Church is the home of Rev. Martin Luther King, Jr's early years of both growing up in the Christian faith and teaching as a pastor. He was baptized here, as well as giving his first sermon at the age of 18! In 1960, he become a co-pastor along with his father, Rev. Martin Luther King, Sr, who was affectionately called "Daddy King". After his assassination in 1968, Martin Luther King, Jr's funeral was held here as a tribute to his spiritual home.

Atlanta GA
HISTORIC EBENEZER
BAPTIST CHURCH

It was in this special place that Rev. King's niece, Dr. Alveda King, shared first hand accounts of some of the family's trials and

tribulations. But what left the most lasting impression on all of us was how the family responded peacefully against overwhelming odds, ultimately changing attitudes around the world.

Birmingham Civil Rights Institute

Dr. King recommended that we drive over to visit The Birmingham Civil Rights Institute, a cultural and education research center that is dedicated to show casing the history of the civil rights movement here in America. They have adopted the adage "those who fail to study from history are doomed to repeat it," by showcasing the evil that can occur when misguided ideology is reinforced and backed up by the actions of the government. The Institute also works diligently to visually explain the dire situations of our past through re-creations

EPISODE 3

and a vivid museum. The Green family is very grateful for the work of the institute, and the teaching of Ahmad Ward, for bringing this history into further perspective.

For more detailed and powerful information, be sure to watch the Extended Learning Scenes with Dr. King and from the museum.

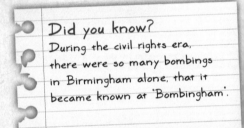

Did you know?
During the civil rights era, there were so many bombings in Birmingham alone, that it became known at "Bombingham".

From Rick's Journal:
This is the first time I've ever felt even remotely close to walking in the shoes of someone else & understanding even a very, very small fraction of the abuse they received. It really hit home when I had to explain these things to my children as we walked through the museum. I'll never be the same. This drastically changed my perspective on race relations. More than ever, I want to be part of the solution.

– Rick

Letter from the Birmingham Jail

In April of 1963, MLK was arrested in Birmingham for demonstrating without a permit. Even though he and others were peacefully protesting over the treatment of the black community, he was jailed for almost a week.

There are few documents which have had as much of an impact on the development of mankind as Rev. Martin Luther King Jr's letter written from the Birmingham Jail. King was able to achieve what most scholars and academics only dream of, penning a document with unquantifiable positive effects on mankind. Rev. King did it all from a jail cell! In addition, every quote that King gave, every philosopher or scripture he cited or referenced, all came from his memory. Unlike most writers, he did not have a vast library to pull information from - he only had his mind. All those years of study and research paid

EPISODE 3

off in a culturally transforming way. We're hoping this made our kids see the greater purpose in all their own studies!

I would encourage everyone to read Dr. King's letter from the Birmingham jail. As Dad was explaining the purpose of the letter and the conditions under which Dr. King wrote it, it left such an impression on me of just how powerful written words for a worthy cause can be. As a song-writer and musician, it made me realize what a positive impact I can have by bringing history alive through music. Dr. King's story truly inspired me!

- Reagan

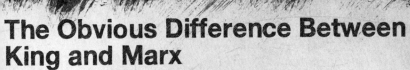

The Obvious Difference Between King and Marx

When we got back home from the trip, we gathered in the living room and reviewed what we had learned. In the Extended Learning Scenes on the DVD's, you can join us in the living room and see how we arrived at our conclusions.

Although he was not the only leader in communist thought, Karl Marx was the foremost formulator of this dangerous and freedom killing ideology. His work, "The Communist Manifesto," written along with Frederick Engels,  details the tenants and principles of communism. These communist principles could not be more contradictory to what Rev. King preached, taught, and lived. In fact, King's good friend and biographer, Lawrence Reddick, when asked this question specifically, said, "There is not a Marxist bone in his body." (referring to King) Even in just the quick research of one episode of our show, we found several key differences between these two men.

EPISODE 3

The first and chief difference between these two individuals is found in religious foundation. Rev. King was a dedicated Christian and his faith informed and influenced everything he did. He was far from perfect and a sinner in need of a Savior just like the rest of us. However, his Christian convictions were not just words, and as such, his social reformations were heavily influenced by the teachings of the Gospel. Marx, on the other hand, viewed Christianity and religion as a whole as not containing any systemic truth, rather, as an institution created by man, for the purpose of man, and relying fully on man. Marx sought to abolition religion, while King sought to spread and live out his faith. These very different foundations caused each man to believe and act in very different ways, even down to their strategies and tactics.

Another difference is their approach to current institutions. Marx was a political radical, desiring to rid the world of many ideals and principles which are imperative to human success. He desired for education to be taken completely away from the parents and given to the state, and for the state

I hereby pledge myself—my person and body—to the nonviolent movement. Therefore I will keep the following ten commandments:

1. Meditate daily on the teachings and life of Jesus.
2. Remember always that the non—violent movement seeks justice and reconciliation — not victory.
3. Walk and talk in the manner of love, for God is love.
4. Pray daily to be used by God in order that all men might be free.
5. Sacrifice personal wishes in order that all men might be free.
6. Observe with both friend and foe the ordinary rules of courtesy.
7. Seek to perform regular service for others and for the world.
8. Refrain from the violence of fist, tongue, or heart.
9. Strive to be in good spiritual and bodily health.
10. Follow the directions of the movement and of the captain on a demonstration.

I sign this pledge, having seriously considered what I do and with the determination and will to persevere.

Name_____
Address_____
Phone_____
Nearest Relative_____
Address_____

Besides demonstrations, I could also help the movement by (Circle the proper items): Run errands, Drive my car, Fix food for volunteers, Clerical work, Make phone calls, Answer phones, Mimeograph, Type, Print Signs, Distribute leaflets.

ALABAMA CHRISTIAN MOVEMENT FOR HUMAN RIGHTS
Birmingham Affiliate of S.C.L.C.
505 1/2 North 17th Street
F.L. Shuttlesworth, President

to completely indoctrinate the child in what the government believed was right and wrong. Marx also was a supporter of eliminating private property, even going so far as to say that "the theory of the Communists may be summed up in a single sentence: The Abolition of Private Property." King, on the other hand, was known for working with current institutions, not abolishing them; seeking to reform, not radicalize. He stood upon and often quoted the Declaration of Independence. While Marx would have sought to replace this founding document full of timeless principles of liberty, King sought its fulfillment. Biographer Reddick said, "Neither by experience nor reading is King a political radical."

The third, and perhaps most glaring difference between King and Marx was that one believed and acted in peace at all costs, while the other used and encouraged violence. While Marx specifically advocated using violence, King expected his fellow protesters to:

"Meditate daily on the teachings and life of Jesus." "Walk and talk in the manner of love, for God is love." "Refrain from the violence of fist, tongue, or heart."

Last, the evidence speaks for itself. Communism is responsible for more than 100 million deaths, while King's peaceful protests led to the liberation and equal treatment under the law for an entire nation.

EPISODE 3

When you compare the two side by side, it is clear that there are no similarities. Our family recommends that everyone read King's Letter from the Birmingham jail, as well as The Communist Manifesto in order to better understand truth, while also being able to identify dangerous ideology.

Kamryn's Final Thoughts:

In the museum we visited, there was a statue of a young girl about my age. Peeking around the edge of a diner, tear running down her cheek, you could see the longing in her eyes to just be accepted, despite the difference in skin  color. Her gaze was glued to two other kids who were not just oblivious to her pain, but were the cause of it, laughing with milkshakes in hand.

This made a hole in my heart, and also taught me the cruelty of being shunned because of something as simple as the color of one's skin.

We don't have to make the same mistakes as previous generations, we can learn from them and do better. Remembering and learning from the past helps us to each be a part of the positive change going forward.

— Kamryn

Discussion Questions

1. Where was Rev. King jailed when he wrote his famous letter

2. Why was Rev. King jailed in the first place?

3. Where did Rev. King preach his first sermon?

4. What nickname did Birmingham receive after this dangerous activity occurred so often?

Essay Question

In your own words and opinion, how are the principles which Rev. Martin Luther King, Jr. taught consistent with the teachings of Christ and the model of American freedom? How do they contrast with communism?

EPISODE 3

Guest Profile:
Dr. Alveda King

Dr. Alveda King is a niece of civil rights leader Rev. Martin Luther King, Jr. and daughter of civil rights activist Rev. A. D. King. Her father and uncle were known as the "sons of thunder" for their powerful preaching. She is an activist, minister, political commentator, author, and former Georgia Legislator. She is a prominent leader within both the religious community and the pro-life movement. We highly recommend her book, King Rules, for both history and great life lessons.

• ALVEDA KING •

KING RULES

TEN TRUTHS FOR YOU, YOUR FAMILY, AND OUR NATION TO PROSPER

Live the Dream of
AD King, Daddy King, and MLK

Special Mention:
Comedy and Constitution Tour

Laugh & Learn with Brad Stine and Rick Green as they use hilarious history to bring America's founding documents to life. During the Comedy and Constitution Tour, Brad and Rick take you through the constitution and the principles of our nation, but in a fun and entertaining way! This tour is perfect for your kids or someone who isn't normally interested in history. They will investigate serious topics during the program, such as the freedoms listed within the 1st Amendment, the importance of Timeless Truth within our founding principles, and you will learn all this while having a side-splitting great time! To book this event or read more, please visit ConstitutionComedy.com.

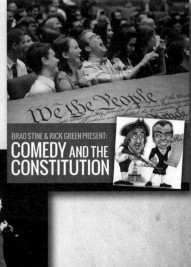

47

A Grateful Nation

There are few topics as emotionally moving as that of our fallen heroes. We have all seen the movies and TV shows like Saving Private Ryan or Band of Brothers. We all respect our veterans, and shudder at the sacrifices that they have gone through. I never fully understood the enormity of what all that meant until we visited Arlington Cemetery. Seeing how many graves there were, seeing just how many people had sacrificed their lives so that I could be free today I was moved. Then, hearing from Col. Birdwell and his story, as well as the dedication of the Honor Guard, I realized These guys are all modern day heroes. When we think of heroes, we think of people from history. But in reality, these heroes are all around us. They are silently standing guard, not caring if they get any fame or attention. By the time we were done with this trip, I realized just how much my respect for them had grown now that I fully understood what they went through and what some of them still go through. We have listed a few of the highlights from the trip below, with some more detailed information on each location. I hope and pray that this information moves you like it moved me.

- Reagan

MARINE CORPS WAR MEMORIAL
DESIGNED 1945, COMPLETED 1954, BY SCULPTOR FELIX DE WELDON.

The Challenge:

Every family should visit Arlington National Cemetery to not only honor the fallen, but inspire the next generation to keep the flame alive.

EPISODE 4

EPISODE 4

Marine Corps War Memorial

The United States Marine Corps War Memorial represents our nation's gratitude to all Marines and those who have fought beside them. The Memorial is dedicated to all Marines who have given their lives for America.

The statue itself replicates Joe Rosenthal's famous photograph of one of the most famous incidents of World War II, the raising of the flag atop Mount Suribachi on Iwo Jima. Despite there being much controversy over the identity of the six marines in the photograph, there is no doubt that we owe a debt to our all Marines that we can only repay by living the freedom for which they sacrificed.

The Marine Corps War Memorial is particularly special to our family because Kara's grand-father actually fought at Iwo Jima and was awarded a Purple Heart for his injuries there.

The State Resolution (right) about Kara's Grandfather (above) was passed by Rick while serving in the Texas House of Representatives.

Arlington National Cemetery

The family was honored to be joined by fellow Texan, Lt. Col. Brian Birdwell, who personally took us on a tour of Arlington National Cemetery and shared the stories of many of the great heroes laid to rest there. The mission of Arlington National Cemetery is "Laying our Nation's veterans...to rest with dignity and honor, while treating their loved ones with respect and compassion." The cemetery accomplishes this goal well for both the veterans buried there, and the visitors who come to honor them. ANC is built on 624 acres that were originally owned by family members of George Washington's wife, Martha Washington. The cemetery is the final resting place for over 400,000 members of our military, and still remains active with funeral services and ceremonies honoring our fallen heroes.

EPISODE 4

Gravesite and The Eternal Flame

One of the things that most impressed the kids was the reverence and respect at the Kennedy eternal flame. Having visited and spoken at Arlington Cemetery multiple times, President John F. Kennedy was buried there, and a memorial erected in his honor. During President Kennedy's funeral, his wife and brother lit the eternal flame that was placed there in honor of his memory. A memorial with some of President Kennedy's most famous quotes was erected around the grave to remind visitors of his words, wisdom, and warnings. So many of these words are still so applicable and inspiring today. We particularly enjoyed the following quote:

> In the long history of the world only a few generations have been granted the role of defending freedom in its hour of maximum danger. I do not shrink from this responsibility, I welcome it!

Audie Murphy

As Texans, we certainly enjoyed learning about one of the most famous Texans to ever live. Audie Leon Murphy was born in Texas on June 20th, 1925, and is the most decorated combat soldier of World War II. He earned 33 awards throughout his career, including the Medal of Honor, The Distinguished Service Cross, and the Silver Star. He was credited with killing over 240 of the enemy, wounding even more, and saving countless of his friends' lives. He fought in 9 major campaigns throughout the war, living through all of them to tell the tales afterwards. After his distinguished military career, Audie returned to the

US to become a successful actor, writer, and even songwriter. He stared in the film "To Hell and Back" detailing the events of his own military career, playing himself! Tragically, Audie passed away on May 28th, 1971, in a plane crash. He was only 45 years of age, yet was already considered to be one of the greatest heroes to ever live.

Tomb of the Unknown Soldier

The Tomb of the Unknown Soldier was established in 1921. The Unknown Soldiers laid to rest at the Tomb represent all missing and unknown service members who made the ultimate sacrifice – they not only gave their lives, but also their identities, to protect these freedoms. On the front of the memorial, it reads **"HERE RESTS IN HONORED GLORY AN AMERICAN SOLDIER KNOWN BUT TO GOD"**. Those words are the final tribute that we can offer the unknown soldiers who died so that we could be free. The memorial itself is guarded by the "Tomb Guard," an extraordinarily disciplined part of the oldest military unit still in service, the 3rd U.S. Infantry Regiment. The guard stays on watch 24/7, as we found out when visiting, regardless of the weather. Their entire mindset can be summed up by Line 6 of their sacred Sentinel's Creed, the code that they all follow, which states, "My

standard will remain perfection"... and it was obvious to us that each guard carried out their duties to perfection!

Final Thoughts:

When we visited the Arlington National Cemetery, it was an emotional day! As I was walking through the cemetery with the graves of soldiers on both sides of me spanning as far as the eye could see, I was overwhelmed with two things.

First, as a mom, I felt extreme gratefulness for the enormous sacrifices made by very young men and women over many generations. The visual of 400,000 graves put everything I love about America into perspective for me, and believe me it will make you emotional!

Second, I felt indignation for all of the criticism that our military endures by loud, ignorant people (that's saying it in a nice way!). It made me think of all the people I've encountered who are so quick to criticize what's wrong about our country, but who have never contributed to the solution. For example, those who don't take the time to even vote... one of the simplest ways to live out our freedom! If you think America's best days are behind her or that the country is so far gone that there's no hope for her, then I encourage you to make it a priority to go to Arlington National Cemetery and walk through those graves and I promise you, you will feel that patriotism swell up in you and you will do whatever it takes to do your part to not let all of those brave soldiers' deaths be in vain! It will be life changing, I promise.

- Kara

Discussion Questions

1. What are the six Marines doing on Iwo Jima in the famous Marine Corps War Memorial?

2. How many fallen members of our military reside in Arlington Cemetery?

3. Who was the most decorated soldier in World War II? How many awards did he receive?

4. What special place does the oldest military unit still in service, the 3rd U.S. Infantry Regiment, protect on a daily basis?

Essay Questions

1. In your own words, what can we do TODAY to honor the sacrifice of our veterans who have given their lives so that we can be free?

2. If you were given the opportunity to speak to war heroes like Col. Brian Birdwell, what would you say?

Guest Profile:
Lt. Col. (Ret) Brian Birdwell

Lt. Col. (Ret.) Brian Birdwell is a decorated military veteran, lifelong Texan, and current State Senator. After his service in our military and his recovery after September 11th, Col. Birdwell and his wife Mel launched "Face the Fire Ministries," a non-profit organization that supports burn survivors, as well as wounded veterans and their families. Col. Birdwell and his wife also authored Refined by Fire: A Family's Triumph of Love and Faith, which chronicles their family's life changing ordeal.

To our family, Col. Brian Birdwell is the definition of a hero. He is our friend, our mentor, and a wonderful man of God. Brian and Mel have one son, Matt, and a fabulous daughter in law, Ann Marie. They reside in Tarrant County, Texas.

Inside
the
Vault

David and Cheryl Barton have long been some of mine and Rick's closest friends and mentors. They have proven themselves to be wonderful examples to us and our kids of how to be effective warriors for Christ here on earth. They have also become the foremost experts in our nation on the history of the Revolutionary War, and the movement to restore our understanding of the founding fathers back to what it used to be. Over the years, they have assembled the largest private collection of founding father documents predating 1812, which has allowed them to conduct extensive research into the truth of what the founding fathers believed. We were very honored that they allowed us to bring our team in to film the magic that resides in their library. It was an experience that we all enjoyed! In this episode, you'll learn powerful secrets about the American founding formula as we discover some of the things that reside inside The Vault!

- Kara

The Adventure:

Experience the entire Revolution and Founding Era in one day at the amazing WallBuilders Library

EPISODE 5

The Mission of WallBuilders and David Barton

WallBuilders is an organization dedicated to presenting America's forgotten history and heroes, with an emphasis on the moral, religious, and constitutional foundation on which America was built. Founded by David Barton, WallBuilders' goal is to exert a direct and positive influence in government, education, and the family by (1) educating the nation concerning the Godly foundation of our country; (2) providing information to federal, state, and local officials as they develop public policies which reflect Biblical values; and (3) encouraging Christians to be involved in the civic arena.

WallBuilders accomplishes these goals through various methods. They are actively developing materials to educate the public concerning the periods in our country's history when its laws and policies were firmly rooted in Biblical principles, so that we can not only have the knowledge to defend the history of our nation, but to implement good policy in today's society. They are also constantly proliferating information and resources that reveal the truth of our nation's past, and making those resources easy to access through their website www.wallbuilders.com and their various public programs. Last, WallBuilders is dedicated to encouraging Christians to enter the public arena and get actively involved. WallBuilders is known nationwide for hosting prayer rallies, weekend information retreats for pastors and legislators, as well as providing tours of our nation's historical sites with an emphasis on their religious history.

WallBuilders is also the home of the largest private collection of founding father documents predating 1812. Their library houses the journals, Bibles, and personal correspondence of some of America's greatest heroes! The writings of great Generals, Presidents, and Pastors all have their home at the WallBuilders Vault.

EPISODE 5

The following is just a small sampling of examples of the hidden history that WallBuilders has been able to preserve and is now using to equip and inspire the citizens of our nation.

John Marshall

At the Vault, WallBuilders has a few pieces of clothing from former Chief Justice of the US Supreme Court, John Marshall. Marshall was born in Virginia on September 24th, 1755, and as a young boy was  heavily influenced by one of his father's friends, George Washington. Marshall served in the Continental Army, eventually earning the rank of Captain. He later studied law at the College of William and Mary and was admitted into the bar. Throughout his life, he served as an American envoy to France, U.S. Congressman, Secretary of State, and eventually  was appointed by President John Adams to be the 4th Chief Justice of the United States Supreme Court. He was unanimously confirmed by the Senate and served as Chief Justice for thirty-four years.

William Ellery

William Ellery was a signer of the Declaration and Delegate from Rhode Island. He was born on December 22nd, 1727. A Harvard graduate and member of the bar, Ellery  served in many public servant positions over the course of his life. He was a member of the Continental Congress, Chief Justice of Rhode Island, as well as many other positions that he filled when needed and called upon. At the Vault, you will see an original pocket watch that belonged to William Ellery.

The Geneva Bible

Getting its name from its late 1500s printing origin in Geneva, Switzerland, this Bible was well known for its endorsement from prominent theologians of the day like John  Calvin and John Knox. It contained both accurate Biblical translations and footnotes towards the back that made clear the lack of Biblical support for the idea of "divine right of kings" when it came to ruling a

EPISODE 5

nation. Considered the most reader friendly bible at its time, the Geneva Bible has gone through a restoration in modern society, with many using it as their main translation of the bible.

The Gun Wad Bible

The Gun Wad Bible was made by Christopher Saur, with the first printing being in 1743 and the third and final being in 1776. The third printing ended up being used by British soldiers, who used the pages as wadding for their muskets, giving the Bible the nickname "The Gun Wad Bible."

Final Thoughts:

It is incredible to me just how much the history of our nation has to do with religion in some form. Whether it be War Bonds or the various Bibles that were so influential, you cannot escape the fact that religion, and Christianity in particular, played a major part in the founding of our nation. I only hope that it continues to be a major pillar for our great nation and future generations.

- Kara

Discussion Questions

1. Who served as the 4th Chief Justice for the United States Supreme Court?

2. Whose pocket watch is on display at the WallBuilders Vault? (Hint: He was a Signer of the Declaration of Independence).

3. Which translation of the Bible was endorsed by theologians like John Calvin and John Knox?

4. Which German translation of the Bible did the family get to hold, most copies of which had been burned or destroyed by the British?

Essay Question

In your own words, why is it important we preserve our nation's history and learn from it in the present?

EPISODE 5

Special Mention:
Wallbuilders Live!

Wallbuilders Live! with David Barton, Rick Green and Tim Barton is a daily journey into the past to capture the ideas of the Founding Fathers of America and then apply them to the major issues of today. Featured guests will include Congressmen, Senators, and other elected officials, as well as experts, activists, authors, and commentators on a variety of issues facing America.

The WallBuilders Library is also the location where David Barton & Rick Green filmed Constitution Alive! A Citizen Guide to the Constitution

Who Shot First?

When I found out we were going to Lexington, Massachusetts to watch the re-enactment of the Battle of Lexington and see Paul Revere ride down the road on his horse warning everyone that the British were coming, I was really excited. I've heard my dad tell this story a thousand times, but honestly there's nothing compared to actually going there and watching these guys dress up and act it out. When we got there, I heard that there was also going to be a 10 mile march in the middle of the night like the real Stow Minutemen did, and I knew that was what I wanted to do because it sounded so cool. The people even offered colonial clothes for us to wear (I'm so glad I don't have to dress like that) and I had to convince my mom that Brad and I could handle it. She finally agreed when Reagan said he would go too, to keep Brad and me out of trouble. Note to self: Listen to my mom next time, because she knows best! :) We also got to visit Reverend Jonas Clark's home. That's where we all got to give our opinion of who we thought shot first, and my dad came prepared with one of Reverend Clark's sermons that pretty much answered the question for us. I'm really glad I got to experience seeing all of the re-enactments, because now when my dad tells the story of the first shot, I can visualize the whole story.

- Rhett

The Facts:

The Lexington Minutemen and the British Regulars faced off in the early morning hours of April 19, 1775. Even to this day, there is much debate about who fired that first shot that was heard around the world.

The Myth:

Did rabble rouser rebels start this battle out of anger? Did someone fire from a hidden position? Or did the British fire first, setting off a course of events they would later regret?

EPISODE 6

Patriot's Day

Patriot's Day is a Massachusetts state holiday that takes place every April commemorating the first battle of the American Revolution fought on April 19th, 1775 in Lexington, Massachusetts. We highly recommend taking your family and witnessing all of the different re-enactments, celebrations, and parades that take place during the week at all times of the day and night. Participating in the festivities and seeing first hand all of the different  events that led up to the "first shot," really brought history to life for us! For our family, this was like going to Disneyworld! There was so much to see and experience and take in with all the re-enactments, that we were practically giddy, feeling like we had stepped back in history! We will hopefully be making another trip in the future to Patriot's Day, because one time is definitely not enough! :)

Hancock – Clark House

We start and end this episode at the historic home often described as a rallying point for patriots, the house of the Reverend Jonas Clark in Lexington, Massachusetts. Members of the Provincial Congress often visited Pastor Clark's home after they began to meet in Concord. It has been known as

an emblem of patriotism since the night of April 18th, 1775. The midnight re-enactment of that famous evening is the beginning of our episode as our family and Brad Stine gathers outside awaiting the arrival of Paul Revere on horseback. He is coming to this specific house to

warn Reverend Clark and his very special houseguests, John Hancock and Sam Adams. It is impossible to describe how much we felt transported back in time as we heard the galloping hooves and then Revere's voice ringing out "THE REGULARS ARE OUT!" (or as the famous poem said, "The British are coming!") As the midnight scene unfolds, Brad Stine asks the big question, "who shot first" to start the war and our quest for an answer began!

The Battle of Lexington

It was only a few hours later in the pre-dawn of April 19th, 1775 when the sound of drums called to arms the men of the

Lexington Militia and they gathered at the triangle shaped common area called "The Green."

Captain John Parker, who led the Minutemen, famously told them, "Don't fire unless fired upon, but if they mean to have war, let it begin here." They stood in the chilling dawn outnumbered 10 to 1 as 800 of His Majesty's Marines, led by Major John Pitcairn, lined up

before them on the same open field. The British troops were on their way to Concord to seize arms and ammunition kept there. For a small farming town with a population of about 800, the British Regulars were an imposing sight. After the seemingly mysterious first shot, the two groups opened

'I hadn't been this excited about a history re-enactment ever in my life. I'd been telling this story for 20 years and now I was about to see it unfold before my eyes! Kara was very concerned I might jump the rope, grab a musket, and join the fight!'

fire on each other. By the time the fight was over, 8 Minutemen were killed and 10 wounded. The Lexington Minutemen, although beat, would later rally together to ambush the British, along with Minutemen from other towns, at a spot now known as "Parker's Revenge."

Reverend Jonas Clark

Reverend Jonas Clark was actively involved in the political workings of our nation prior to the famous battle at the Lexington Green, even going so far as to persuade his parishioners to burn their tea on the Lexington Green in protest to the Stamp Act, three days before the now famous Boston Tea Party! He was known as a leading patriot minister, and was respected by the leaders of the revolution. Many say it was his fiery sermons on liberty that primed the guns of the Revolution. It was because of his passionate patriotism that men like John Hancock and Samuel Adams sought safety within his home. Because of his dedication to our country, Rev. Clark was given the honor of delivering the Election sermon to the legislature elected in 1781 under the new constitution.

EPISODE 6

Rev. Clark's sermon on the one-year anniversary of the "shot heard round the world" is a detailed and thorough defense of the Minutemen, and he makes a very strong case for the British being the ones to have fired first.

Excerpted from Rev. Clark's Sermon:

As to the question, "Who fired first?," if it can be a question with anyone; we may observe, that though General Gage hath been pleased to tell the world in his account of this savage transaction, "that the troops were fired upon by the rebels out of the meetinghouse and the neighbouring houses, as well as by those that were in the field; and that the troops only returned the fire and passed on their way to Concord;" yet nothing can be more certain than the contrary, and nothing more false, weak, or wicked than such a representation. To say nothing of the absurdity of the supposition, "that 50, 60, or even 70 men, should, in the open field, commence hostilities with 1200 or 1500 of the best troops of Britain," nor of the known determination of this small party of Americans, upon no consideration whatever, to begin the scene of blood. A cloud of witnesses, whose veracity cannot be justly disputed, upon oath have declared in the most express and positive terms, "that the British

troops fired first ." And, I think, we may safely add, without the least reason or provocation. Nor was there opportunity given for our men to have saved themselves, either by laying down their arms or dispersing, as directed, had they been disposed to; as the command to fire upon them was given almost at the same instant that they were ordered, by the British officers, to disperse and to lay down their arms, &c. In short, so far from firing first upon the king's troops; upon the most careful enquiry, it appears that but very few of our people fired at all; and even they did not fire 'till after being fired upon by the troops, they were wounded themselves, or saw others killed or wounded by them, and looked upon it next to impossible for them to escape. As to any firing from the meetinghouse, as Gage represents; it is certain, that there

were but four men in the meetinghouse when the troops came up: and they were then getting some ammunition from the town stock and had not so much as loaded their guns (except one, who never discharged it) when the troops fired upon the militia. And as to the neighbouring houses, it is equally

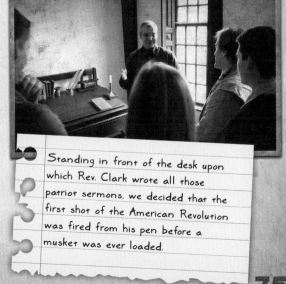

Standing in front of the desk upon which Rev. Clark wrote all those patriot sermons, we decided that the first shot of the American Revolution was fired from his pen before a musket was ever loaded.

certain that there was no firing from them, unless, after the dispersion of our men, some who had fled to them for shelter, might fire from them upon the troops. One circumstance more, before the brigade quitted Lexington, I beg leave to mention, as what may give a further specimen of the spirit and character, of the officers and men of this body of troops. After the militia company were dispersed and the firing ceased, the troops drew up and formed in a body on the common, fired a volley and gave three huzzas by way of triumph and as expressive of the joy of victory and glory of conquest! Of this transaction I was a witness, having at that time a fair view of their motions and being at the distance of not more than 70 or 80 rods from them. Whether this step was honorary to the detachment, or agreeable to the rules of war, or how far it was expressive of bravery, heroism and true military glory, for 800 disciplined troops of Great Britain, without notice or provocation, to fall upon 60 or 70 undisciplined Americans, who neither opposed nor molested them, and murder some and disperse the rest, and then to give the shout and make the triumph of victory, is not for me to determine, but must be submitted to the impartial world to judge. That "there is a God with whom is the power, and the glory, and the victory," is certain: but whether He will set His seal to the triumph made upon this most peculiar occasion, by following it with further successes and, finally giving up this people into the hands of those that have thus cruelly commenced hostilities against them, must be left to time to discover.

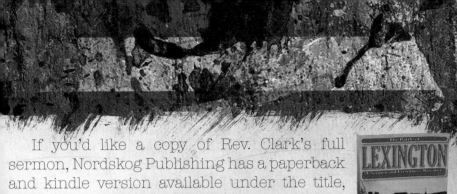

If you'd like a copy of Rev. Clark's full sermon, Nordskog Publishing has a paperback and kindle version available under the title, The Battle of Lexington: A Sermon And Eyewitness Narrative, and it can be purchased at Nordskogpublishing.com

Stow Minutemen

While Trey, Kamryn, Rick, & Kara were waiting in the early morning darkness for the Lexington re-enactment to begin, Rhett, Reagan, and Brad were literally marching all night with another group of Minutemen re-enactors for the 10 mile walk to Concord. Before the revolutionary war began, The Provincial Congress requested that 1/3-1/2 of each town's militia be selected to serve and be called upon at a minutes notice in the case of an emergency, giving them the name "Minutemen." Although little can be confirmed from that night, what is known is that 80 men of Stow grouped together to face the British at the Battle of Concord, with hope of avenging their brothers from Lexington. While the Green boys and Brad didn't get much sleep, they got a first hand lesson in marching

The march from Stow to Concord is almost 9 miles and takes about 4 hours.

for freedom and even learned a little about the modern day infringements on the 2nd Amendment.

The New Minuteman Company was reactivated in 1966 to promote interest in Revolutionary history.

Captain John Parker

John Parker was born on July 13th, 1729, in Lexington, Massachusetts. As a veteran of the French and Indian War, Parker was dedicated to his country and volunteered to lead the local minutemen in Lexington. After the French and Indian War, Parker was a farmer, mechanic, and held various local political positions. Although he participated in the beginning of the Revolutionary War, little is known about his activities or the particular battles in which he fought. He passed away from illness on September 17th, 1775.

What I Learned:

It must have been hard for those Minutemen to leave the warmth and comfort of their homes in the middle of the night, knowing that they were marching to stand against a powerful army. It was hard enough on us just marching in the cold and taking breaks to drink hot chocolate! I also really liked learning about Pastor Clark and how he was the one that inspired the local people to understand why liberty was worth fighting for. Finally, I learned that Uncle Brad would not have been a very good Minuteman unless he had some minions like Reagan and me to carry him everywhere.

— Rhett

EPISODE 6

Rick's Final Thoughts:

1. The Minutemen were literally ready to lay down their lives at a moment's notice. They didn't complain, they didn't give excuses, they just followed orders and did what needed to be done. Sometimes we are asked to simply move into action quickly when called upon, so it's better to make up our minds now that we will do what needs to be done when the time comes.

2. Sometimes we don't see the fruits of our actions. We may not enjoy the reward for which we are sacrificing. For the 8 men who died at Lexington, some at the time very well might have thought that they died for nothing; but history shows us that their sacrifice was the beginning of our revolution.

3. Being prepared helps! The Minutemen were only able to take a stand and fight the British Regulars off at Concord because they had taken time out of their lives to train and prepare. We need to be willing to train ourselves in whatever our calling is, so that we can step up when needed.

BATTLE GREEN / Lexington

Discussion Questions

1. Who led the British troops at the Battle of Lexington?

2. Who led the Minutemen at the Battle of Lexington?

3. Who stayed at Reverend Jonas Clark's house and was warned that the British were coming to get them?

4. Who brought the warning on horseback about the British coming to Lexington?

5. What were the British troops planning to do once they had reached Concord?

Essay Question

Who do you believe most likely fired the first shot? Why do you believe your conclusion?

Changing Seasons

We started off our road trip to Virginia with a lot of excitement for Trey's graduation at Liberty University. Knowing how hard he worked to get to that point, made my momma's heart so proud of him. We wanted to soak in our time with him and make the most of our trip by making some stops along the way that incorporated history and life lessons. Learning about the life of pastor Samuel Davies and John Peter Gabriel Muhlenberg were a perfect addition to the trip. I think the pastors of the Revolutionary period played such important roles in our history. Muhlenberg was a minister for a season and then a soldier for another season. We try to teach our kids that God may call you to changing seasons of your life and that's ok, and no matter what your "profession" is, you can impact your community, your state, and nation. Just be ready to answer the call. Learning from the heroes of history is so inspiring to us. There are stories upon stories of patriots young and old who lived ordinary lives and then stepped up to fulfill their calling when the time was right. I'm thankful that all you have to do to find a hero is look back in history!

- Kara

The Adventure:

While traveling to Lynchburg, Virginia, Rick tries to squeeze in as many historic stops as possible as the family learns about Changing Seasons.

Historic Polegreen Church in Virginia

On the way to Trey's graduation ceremony, our family stopped by a few key historical locations to try and drive home a few life lessons during this season of change. The first of these was the memorial to Polegreen Church, also known as the Hanover Meeting House, which was destroyed in the mid 1800s. Even though the building is gone, the history that exists within the memorial was powerful and moving.

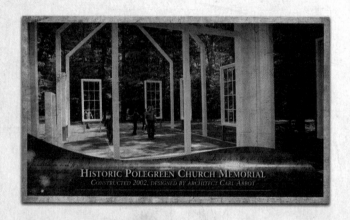

HISTORIC POLEGREEN CHURCH MEMORIAL
CONSTRUCTED 2002, DESIGNED BY ARCHITECT CARL ABBOT

Originally licensed in 1743, the Hanover Meeting House was the home of quite a few American heroes. It was originally licensed at a time when the Government of the area protected an official denomination (The Anglican Church) and discouraged other religions from gathering for worship. The Hanover Meeting House was one of just four places that

were originally licensed as "reading houses" under different denominations. All four places that were licensed to preach decided to bring in a 23-year-old Presbyterian minister by the name of Samuel Davies.

Samuel Davies

In 1747, Samuel Davies became the first non-Anglican minister licensed to preach in Virginia. He became prominently known for his contributions to the religious and political climates of the colony, his education of black slaves, and his mentorship of Founding Fathers like Patrick Henry. Henry grew up listening to Davies preach at the Polegreen church each Sunday, and was then required by his mom to recite each sermon back to her on their trip home. Henry greatly admired Rev. Davies' preaching and eloquence as a teacher, and credited Davies with "teaching me what an orator should be." When Davies passed away in 1761, his sermons were well known and influenced how other clergy preached at the time. By the time the Revolution began years later, his sermons were among the most widely circulating collections of sermons in the colonies.

Rev. Davies had a heart for teaching slaves how to read, because if they could read, then they could understand the Bible, and that was his goal. He was really a trail-blazer because he did the things that no one before him was willing to do.

Rev. Davies was also heavily involved in the education system, becoming the 4th President of Princeton University, where he raised the standards for admission and for the bachelor's degree and instituted monthly orations by members of the senior class. Isn't it incredible how religious our early education institutions were?

Emmanuel Church

The next stop for the family was at Emmanuel Church in Woodstock, Virginia. While it is not the original building in which **John Peter Gabriel Muhlenberg** preached in, his congregation built this church after their

original building was destroyed. To honor Muhlenberg, the congregation incorporated words in memory of him on one of their windows. Not only is the church beautiful, but you could feel the history as you walked through the sanctuary. The true treasure of the trip was getting the chance to flip through Muhlenberg's Bible, the very one from which he preached his famous "seasons" sermon. From the pulpit Rev. Muhlenberg often preached on the principles of liberty, preparing his congregation for the day they could be called on to support the

cause of freedom. In January of 1776, Rev. Muhlenberg preached a farewell sermon to his congregation from Ecclesiastes 3, *"To every thing there is a season, and a time to every purpose under Heaven, a time to be born, and a time to*

die... A time to weep, and a time to laugh... A time of war, and a time of peace. It is a time for war!... It is time to act! Many of us came to this country to practice our religious freedoms. It is time to fight for those freedoms that we hold so dear... I am a clergyman, it is true. But I am also a patriot — and my liberty is as dear to me as to any man. Shall I hide behind my robes, sitting still at home, while others spill their blood to protect my freedom? Heaven forbid it! I am called by my country to its defense. The cause is just and noble. I am convinced it is my duty to obey that call, a duty I owe to my God and to my country. In the language of the holy writ, there was a time for all things, a time to preach and a time to pray but those times have passed away. There is a time to fight, and that time has come now!"

At the end of his sermon he threw off his clerical robes to reveal a full military uniform. That day, it is said that he recruited 300 men from his congregation to join him in becoming the 8th Virginia Brigade.

EPISODE 7

There is nothing more exciting for us as a family than when we get the chance to actually see original documents or artifacts that date as far back as the Revolutionary War. To see and read from

EMMANUEL CHURCH
Woodstock, Virginia

Muhlenberg's treasured Bible, while learning about the man himself, was a once in a lifetime opportunity.

John Peter Gabriel Muhlenberg

John Muhlenberg, a patriot pastor, accomplished many things in his life. Before he was a well-known Lutheran minister, he had actually served with a German regiment of dragoons in the 1760s. That experience allowed him to raise his own regiment of troops in the Revolutionary War and be commissioned a Brigadier General in the Continental Army by the end of the war. He not only fought for freedom during the war, he lived for it afterward as well. He served in many political positions in order to refine and protect the freedom that he had fought and sacrificed for. He was a member of the Continental Congress, served in State

"A TIME TO PREACH, AND A TIME TO FIGHT"
STATUE OF MAJOR GENERAL PETER MUHLENBERG BY J. OTTO SCHWEIZER, 1910

positions, and was even appointed by President Thomas Jefferson to the supervisor of revenue for all of Pennsylvania. He also worked closely with his younger brother...

Frederick Augustus Conrad Muhlenberg

Frederick Muhlenberg was a Lutheran minister who preached for most of his early life. Frederick Augustus was a pastor at a Lutheran church in New York, and he strongly disagreed with his brother's outspoken view on politics from the pulpit.

Frederick wrote to John Peter saying, *"You have become too involved in matters which, as a preacher, you have nothing whatsoever to do..."*.

John Peter responded back to his brother by stating, *"I am a Clergyman it is true, but I am a member of the Society as well as the poorest Layman, and my Liberty is as dear to me as any man, shall I then sit still and enjoy myself at home when the best blood of the continent is spilling?"*

John Peter even accused his brother of being a Tory sympathizer.

EPISODE 7

Frederick Muhlenberg then saw the devastating side of war up close when the British desecrated his church in New York and he and his family were forced to flee the city and move deep into the Pennsylvania countryside. However, after two more years of continual unrest, Frederick had a change of heart and joined the patriotic cause and went on to be involved as a

BROTHERS UNITED

FREDERICK MUHLENBERG BECAME THE FIRST SIGNER OF THE BILL OF RIGHTS ON SEPTEMBER 28, 1791, 15 YEARS AFTER HIS BROTHER PETER PREACHED THE FAMOUS SERMON IN WOODSTOCK, VIRGINIA.

member of the Continental Congress, the State House of Representatives, and eventually was elected the first Speaker of the House for the new American Government.

Brothers and pastors, these two men started off with very different opinions and paths, but ended up serving in Congress together helping pass the First Amendment that now protects our religious liberty.

Graduation

Trey completed his entire B.A. in Economics in just 18 months. He earned 42 hours in his final three months through a combination of online classes, CLEP tests, and his senior level classes at

Liberty University. Liberty is the largest private university in America and the largest Christian University in the world. Located on more than 7,000 acres in Lynchburg, Virginia, Liberty offers 450 programs from the certificate to the doctoral level, and is the home to more than 100,000 residential and online students. Of the more than 17,000 graduates in Trey's class, he was the youngest at 17 years of age. After watching Trey work so hard to accomplish such a big goal, we were all excited for him to say the least!

EPISODE 7

Closing Thoughts:

I'm so intrigued by the story of the Muhlenberg brothers. It reminds me how there's truly nothing new under the sun. Even today, many families and friends are often very much on opposite sides of political and religious issues. I'm grateful though that John Peter & Frederick were willing to recognize the changing seasons in their lives and follow His calling, wherever that took them. That is something that we have tried to instill in our kids. If you have a dream or goal and God gets you there, hold that dream loosely in your hand, because if that season of your life changes and you are called to something different, you won't be disappointed to let that dream go.

- Kara

Discussion Questions

1. What roles did Pastors play in the Founding Era that you learned about in this episode?

2. Why did Samuel Davies want to teach slaves how to read?

3. Name the two pastors that the Green Family learned about on this trip. Name one thing you learned about each.

4. Which scripture did John Peter Muhlenberg preach from that called his men to arms right after his sermon?

Essay Question

Do you think pastors today should be as outspoken from the pulpit about politics as John Peter Gabriel Muhlenberg was? Do you think pastors should have the right to speak openly about candidates from the pulpit?

The Crossing

The Crossing of the Delaware is one of the most inspirational stories in America's history. In this episode, our family takes you on a little trip through some of the most influential moments of history and the shaping of our nation. You'll come along for the ride with us as we experience Valley Forge, Carpenters Hall, and even the very spot where General George Washington led what little remained of his army across that icy Delaware River and then nine miles (some of them bare foot) through the snow. Many know Washington as the father of the country, but something most people don't know is how important his faith was. Washington was truly a man of great stature, but it only happened because of his faith in God, time in prayer, and putting his life in God's hands daily. Throughout this episode, we learn just how often Washington was on his knees before God. This episode is a journey about faith, duty, and responsibility. I hope you get as much out of it as I did! I'd encourage you to actually go visit these sights and see them with your own eyes. There is nothing quite like walking in the footsteps of our Founders.

- Reagan

The Adventure:

Dad starts the family off with a "wager" to get us hunting down historic clues and we end up tracing the footsteps (and kneeling places) of George Washington from before the War to the impossible "crossing" on Christmas Day.

EPISODE 8

EPISODE 8

Carpenters' Hall

Carpenters' Hall is rich in American history. It was home to the First Continental Congress in 1774, it housed Benjamin Franklin's Library Company, and even The First and Second Banks

of the United States. It has continuously been owned by the oldest trade guild in America, The Carpenters' Company, and was frequently loaned out to be used by various organizations that needed a space to meet.

CONTINENTAL CONGRESS
A convention of delegates called together from the thirteen colonies.
The first Continental Congress assembled September 5, 1774,
at Carpenters' Hall in Philadelphia, Pennsylvania.
Twelve of the thirteen colonies sent delegates to the convention.

Just as Rich pointed out in the episode, the first meeting of the Continental Congress was an indicator of just how religious the Founding Fathers were. Reverend Jacob Duché was invited to minister to the group, which resulted in a three-hour prayer and Bible study

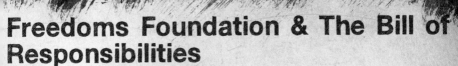

Freedoms Foundation & The Bill of Responsibilities

The Freedoms Foundation at Valley Forge was founded upon The American Credo, written by General (and later President) Dwight D. Eisenhower. Eisenhower's Credo was a set of philosophical principles, which he believed were fundamental to the organization and the nation. Within this Credo, President Eisenhower started off by saying some of the most important principles were:

FREEDOMS FOUNDATION, VALLEY FORGE

Founded in 1949, Freedoms Foundation is built on land that was once a part of General George Washington's famous encampment of Valley Forge.

1. Political and economic rights which protect the dignity and freedom of the individual
2. Constitutional government designed to serve the people
3. Fundamental belief in God

It is difficult to believe that God has no place in our government when our greatest heroes like President Eisenhower have credited so much to Him, and placed such importance on a fundamental belief in Him.

The Freedoms Foundation later expanded upon this creed with their Bill of Responsibilities, the Preamble to which reads:

EPISODE 8

Freedom and responsibility are mutual and inseparable; we can ensure enjoyment of the one only by exercising the other. "Freedom for all of us depends on responsibility by each of us. To secure and expand our liberties, therefore, we accept these responsibilities as individual members of a free society."

Once again, the Freedoms Foundation makes clear that in order to effectively act upon these lists of imperative responsibilities, a fundamental belief in God must exist.

Scan this QR code to download your own copy of the Bill of Responsibilities!

Bill of Responsibilities

Preamble. Freedom and responsibility are mutual and inseparable; we can ensure enjoyment of the one only by exercising the other. Freedom for all of us depends on responsibility by each of us. To secure and expand our liberties, therefore, we accept these responsibilities as individual members of a free society:

- To be fully responsible for our own actions and for the consequences of those actions. Freedom to choose carries with it the responsibility for our choices.

- To respect the rights and beliefs of others. In a free society, diversity flourishes. Courtesy and consideration toward others are measures of a civilized society.

- To give sympathy, understanding and help to others. As we hope others will help us when we are in need, we should help others when they are in need.

- To do our best to meet our own and our families' needs. There is no personal freedom without economic freedom. By helping ourselves and those closest to us to become productive members of society, we contribute to the strength of the nation.

- To respect and obey the laws. Laws are mutually accepted rules by which, together, we maintain a free society. Liberty itself is built on a foundation of law. That foundation provides an orderly process for changing laws. It also depends on our obeying laws once they have been freely adopted.

- To respect the property of others, both private and public. No one has a right to what is not his or hers. The right to enjoy what is ours depends on our respecting the right of others to enjoy what is theirs.

- To share with others our appreciation of the benefits and obligations of freedom. Freedom shared is freedom strengthened.

- To participate constructively in the nation's political life. Democracy depends on an active citizenry. It depends equally on an informed citizenry.

- To help freedom survive by assuming personal responsibility for its defense. Our nation cannot survive unless we defend it. Its security rests on the individual determination of each of us to help preserve it.

- To respect the rights and to meet the responsibilities on which our liberty rests and our democracy depends. This is the essence of freedom. Maintaining it requires our common effort, all together and each individually.

Freedoms Foundation
at Valley Forge
1601 Valley Forge Road, P.O. Box 706
Valley Forge, PA 19482-0706
610-933-8825 • Fax: 610-935-0522 • E-mail: ffvf@ffvf.org • www.ffvf.org

The Crossing of the Delaware River

It was a cold and dreary Christmas night in December of 1776, in Trenton, New Jersey, when Washington made the decision to cross the icy Delaware River and catch the Hessian troops off guard. Many said it couldn't be done and that it was a tactical mistake. The Hessians were settling in for the winter with no

expectation of fighting again until spring. They had no idea a surprise attack from Washington was about to happen. Washington had faith in his decision, he had faith that his men would be protected, and he had faith there would be a much-needed victory. Even though Washington's troops were hungry, under clothed, and malnourished, they were so loyal to their leader that they were willing to follow him across an icy river, walk 9 miles in the snow, and take on mercenaries - literally professional hired guns. The Hessian mercenaries were highly regarded and sought after, with a large amount of fighting experience under their belt. They totaled 1,400 troops waiting nine miles on the other side of the river across from Washington.

The crossing of the river itself was a feat that should not have been possible, let alone defeating the Hessian army. When they crossed the river and attacked the Hessians, the Hessians were on high alert, but exhausted from constant patrolling. Washington had been skirmishing and harassing the Hessians in the surrounding countryside, forcing them to keep alert. Because of his foresight and tactics, when Washington attacked the Hessians, they were exhausted and surrendered within a single hour.

The crossing of the Delaware River was a tremendous feat, one that will remain in our minds as tactical brilliance on the part of Washington. His foresight combined with his reliance on Divine Providence was a combination even the professional mercenaries could not withstand.

Take Home Lesson:

There is convincing evidence that when God chooses, he can change the course of history. This does not mean we should neglect our duty to do our best, or shirk from our responsibility. We are God's hands and feet, here to accomplish

His purpose. Just like Washington prepared his fight against the Hessians through brilliant tactics, we also must prepare ourselves throughout life in all that we do. Remember the words of President John Quincy Adams, Duty is ours, results are God's.

- Reagan

Discussion Questions

1. Where did the First Continental Congress meet?

2. Who opened in prayer for the First Continental Congress?

3. For how long did the prayer and Bible study last during the First Continental Congress?

4. What group of soldiers were defeated by Washington after he crossed the Delaware River?

5. What principle is the bedrock and foundation of the bill of responsibilities?

Essay Question

In your own words, would it be beneficial to society for the bill of responsibilities to be actively lived out? How would you personally best live them out?

Come & Take It!

This week's episode takes us to the iconic Battle of the Alamo and the lesser known, but even more critical, part of the Texas Revolution...Gonzales! To set up this episode appropriately, we need to go back more than just a few hundred years, we need to step back a couple thousand years.

When the Persians demanded surrender of the 300 Spartans at the battle of Thermopylae in 480 BC, Leonidas responded with "MONAN LABE!!!" Which is, to say in English - "Come and Take it!" And then they made their heroic stand against an impossibly larger force of Persians.

More than 2,300 years later, that same phrase and attitude became the battle cry against tyranny in our family's home state of Texas.

What started as a simple ribbon cutting for our family's newly renovated historic hotel, became a challenge to defend the courage of some of the greatest men in history.

We begin with the chaos of the grand opening for The Alcalde Hotel, when Brad (a Tennessean) decides to question whether our Texas icons were heroes or cowards. This leads to a journey through the first shots of the Texas Revolution, the story behind that white flag with the cannon, the Alamo in San Antonio, and the amazing story of the Immortal Thirty-Two. Somewhere in the mix, we get to shoot muskets with a very authentic re-enactor...and guess who gets off the best shot?

- Rick

The Question:

Was the courageous last stand at the Alamo just a myth? Were there cowards fleeing from the Alamo?

Gonzales

Our episode begins in the city of Gonzales, located just southeast of Austin, the Texas Capitol. Gonzales is a town rich in history, with the first shot of the Texas revolution occurring

here. Rick represented Gonzales in the Texas Legislature from 1999-2003 and had it officially named "The Lexington of Texas" for her "first shot" history. Having a little over 7,000 people, Gonzales is exactly what comes to mind when you think of a small town in Texas!

Alcalde Hotel

The Alcalde Hotel originally opened in 1926 and served the Gonzales area with rooms as well as a coffee shop and dining room. The Alcalde is filled with history and folk lore. Bonnie & Clyde once stayed at the Alcalde, escaping out the window and

climbing down a tree when the local law showed up. Elvis Presley stayed at the Alcalde multiple times during his days as part of the Louisiana Hay Ride. Our family has since renovated the Alcalde to a beautiful hotel and grill.

For more information, visit www.TheAlcaldeHotel.com. Come stay with us next time you come through Texas!

First Shot

Before the famous Battle at the Alamo, was the little known **Battle of Gonzales**, the first military engagement in the war for Texas independence. Originally, the Mexican government had loaned

the settlers of Gonzales a cannon for the purpose of fending off Indians. In 1835, the president of Mexico, Santa Anna, overthrew the Mexican Constitution and appointed himself dictator. Santa Anna feared that his dictatorship would push the Texians to secede from Mexico, so he ordered the Mexican military to start disarming the Texians whenever possible. Santa Anna then sent 100 Mexican dragoons to retrieve the

cannon from the Gonzales settlers that had been loaned to them four years earlier. The citizens of Gonzales refused to give up the cannon, and decided to take a stand against the Mexican dragoons (YES!).

EPISODE 9

While it was originally just 18 Gonzales townsmen, more militiamen from surrounding settlements were summoned, resulting in a small group of nearly 140 men to stand against the dragoons.

The Texians ultimately attacked the Mexicans and refused to give up the cannon, resulting in the dragoons re-treating from the fight. This was officially the "first shot". The battle itself was a minor affair, but it represented the first real act of war on the part of the settlers, and was therefore a major step forward in the movement to throw off the chains of the tyrannical Mexican government. **The Battle of Gonzales** was to Texas what the Battle of Lexington was for the United States. **The Battle of Gonzales** sparked the flame of liberty in the hearts and minds of all Texians, causing many of them to go into action and resist the tyranny of Santa Anna and the Mexican government. From this battle, the now famous "Come and Take It" flag was born. After the Battle of Gonzales, the Texians fought many battles for another six months, before finally achieving independence!

First shots fired in Gonzales.
Oct 2, 1835
September October November December January February March

The Alamo

The Battle of the Alamo is the most famous battle that occurred during the fight for Texas Independence. It was a thirteen-day siege, ending with a major defeat for the  Texian defenders by the Mexican army. The Texians were commanded by Lt. Col. William B. Travis.

Travis knew that they desperately needed reinforcements, and inside the Alamo he penned one of the most stirring letters in American history pleading for the people of Texas and all Americans in the world to aid them in this battle. Even despite being outnumbered and knowing that death was likely, Travis wrote:

> "The enemy has demanded a surrender at discretion
> – I have answered the demand with a cannon shot &
> our flag still waves proudly from the walls – I shall
> never surrender or retreat."

You can see why we Texans have a lot of pride in our state! Words like that stir up a lot of patriotism for the cause of liberty! Travis's letter was immediately dispatched out and word of it spread as far as New York City. Responding to his letter were thirty-two brave men from Gonzales, called the Immortal 32.

Nearly 2,000 Mexican soldiers continually attempted to break through the 200 defenders of the Alamo. On March 6, 1836, after thirteen days, the Mexicans made a final assault on the weary Texians killing all of them in a bloody battle that lasted about ninety minutes, while losing around 600 men themselves. William B. Travis, David Bowie, and even the famous frontiersman and former Congressman, David Crockett (known as "King of the Wild Frontier") died that day defending the Alamo. A few civilians were spared by Santa Anna and sent away to warn the remainder of the Texian forces that his Mexican army was unbeatable. Santa Anna chose to make an example out of the brave soldiers at the Alamo, and even though the defeat that day sent fear through many Texians,

TEXT OF THE TRAVIS LETTER:

Commandancy of the Alamo--

Bejar Fby. 24th 1836

To the People of Texas &
all Americans in the world--

Fellow citizens & compatriots--

I am besieged, by a thousand or more of the Mexicans under Santa Anna ----- I have sustained a continual Bombardment & cannonade for 24 hours & have not lost a man ----- The enemy has demanded a Surrender at discretion, otherwise, the garrison are to be put to the sword, if the fort is taken ----- I have answered the demand with a cannon shot, & our flag still waves proudly from the wall ----- Ishall never Surrender or retreat

Then, I can on you in the name of Liberty, of patriotism & every thing dear to the American character, to come to our aid, with an dispatch ----- The enemy is receiving reinforcements daily &will no doubt Increase to three or four thousand in four or five days. If this can is neglected, I am deter mined to sustain myself as long as possible & die like a soldier who never forgets what is due to his own honor & that of his country ----- Victory or Death

William Barret Travis
Lt. Col. Comdt

P. S. The lord is on our side-When the enemy appeared in sight we had not three bushels of corn--- We have since found in deserted houses 80 or 90 bushels & got into the walls 20 or 30 head of Beeves---

it also created a thirst for revenge. **"Remember the Alamo"** became a rallying cry across Texas, and Santa Anna himself was captured at The Battle of San Jacinto, less than sixty days after the fall of the Alamo. Treaties were signed May 14th, formal surrender of the Mexican Army was June 4th, and The Republic of Texas was   a free and independent nation just eight months from the firing of the first shot in Gonzales.

The Immortal Thirty-Two

During the siege at the Alamo, Col. Travis sent several requests for aid, his most famous being the "Victory or Death" letter of February 24, 1836.

The only known answer to Travis's call for help came in the form of the Immortal Thirty-Two from Gonzales. They not only answered the call, they fought their way through the Mexican forces in order to get into the Alamo and aid the defenders. Although they knew death was likely, they did not shrink from their responsibility to their fellow Texians, but instead, they welcomed it. These Immortal Thirty-Two, along with the rest of the defenders of the Alamo, were true heroes of courage.

The Answer:

The men of the Alamo were most definitely not cowards! They not only stood their ground, they ran towards the fight!

Take Home Lessons:

It started with only 18 brave men willing to say "no more." That small band of patriots knew they were standing against the entire, seemingly impossible to overcome, Mexican Army when they began their stance.

We are given so many opportunities to take a stand every day. Whether it's simply speaking up for truth in a small circle of friends, or perhaps even standing up for the defenseless in our communities. Your "stand" may be with your vote, or a letter to the editor, or a post on Facebook. For some of you, it will be joining the military and defending our nation physically, or serving as a first responder in your community. But for all of us, whether simply using our voices or literally laying down our lives, there is no limit to the potential impact we can have on the future of liberty in our great nation. Others will rally to the cause if just a few, or sometimes even one, is willing to raise the flag and say, "Come and Take It!"

— Rick

Discussion Questions

1. Name a famous individual that stayed at the Alcalde Hotel?

2. Why was a contingent of Mexican dragoons sent to Gonzales?

3. How many Mexican troops attacked the Alamo?

4. How long did the siege of the Alamo last?

5. Who were the only people to answer Col. Travis's call for aid at the Alamo?

Essay Question

What is a specific way that you and your family can stand for truth and use your voice to rally others to do their part as free citizens to protect and pass liberty to the next generation?

EPISODE 9

Guest Profile:
Dr. Bruce Winders

We had such a great time with Dr. Bruce Winders and learned so much in our time with him at the Alamo. Dr. Winders earned his doctorate at Texas Christian University in Fort Worth, Texas in 1994. He came to the Alamo in 1996 to fill the newly created position of Historian & Curator. A recognized authority on the conflicts involving United States, Mexico, and Texas, Winders is the author of a number of books and articles on the topic, including Mr. Polk's Army: The American Military Experience in the Mexican War (1997), Crisis in the Southwest: The United States, Mexico, and the Struggle over Texas (2002), Sacrificed at the Alamo: Tragedy and Triumph in the Texas Revolution (2004), and Panting for Glory: The Mississippi Rifles in the Mexican War (2016). A former classroom teacher and public historian, Winders maintains a keen interest in education and educators. Those who know him can readily attest to his passion and skill as an educator of students of all ages. Be sure to watch the Extended Learning Scenes on the DVD's for more time at the Alamo with Dr. Winders.

Dr. Bruce Winders

Alamo Historian and Curator
Author of 'Sacrificed at the Alamo:
Tragedy and Triumph in the
Texas Revolution'

Guest Profile:
George Rollow

Special thanks to Texas Revolution re-enactor George Rollow for giving us a great experience shooting muskets and also sharing some wonderful history with us. Be sure to watch the Extended Learning Scenes on the DVD's for some extra learning and shooting!

George Rollow

Texas History Reenactor
Colonel, Texas Army

Midnight Riders

We start off this episode at the Patterson's ranch, the founders of Boss Your Heart Orphan Ministry. Kamryn and I got to ride horses and we had such a great time. That night, as we were sitting around the campfire back at home, a question was raised: "Who was the better midnight Rider, Paul Revere or Sybil Ludington?" CHALLENGE ACCEPTED. And that's what started the crazy adventure of Kamryn and me learning as much as we could about Paul Revere and Sybil Ludington. I took a team to Boston, where Paul Revere lived, and we learned of the courage and sacrifice Paul Revere had to make during that midnight ride. Kamryn and my dad drove over to Carmel, New York to discover the bravery and commitment of Sybil Ludington. It felt like a Red Sox & Yankees rivalry already! After a lot of research (and some fun with Uncle Brad), it was time to write a speech and give it at Dad's Comedy & Constitution event. Now you get to come along for the ride. (see what I did there?)

- Rhett

The Question:

Who made the greater Midnight Ride?
Sybil Ludington or Paul Revere?

Paul Revere Monument
Boston North End, MA

EPISODE 10

EPISODE 10

As a family, we strongly believe that competition has the ability to bring out the best in everyone, and that it gives each person the chance to grow in their abilities and knowledge. For this trip,

Kamryn and Rhett got to experience a little competition while learning some really cool things about Paul Revere and Sybil Ludington.

We started off in Boston, a city filled with great history and great baseball. Normally, our family would always fit in time for a game at Fenway Park to see the Red Sox, but on this trip there was so much to cover that we actually had to split up and go different directions. Rick took Kamryn to follow up on her research of the little known Sybil Ludington, while Rhett had mapped out several Paul Revere landmarks and took Mom and Reagan along for the ride. Trey was off studying for law school exams and had to pick up Brad from the airport for the Comedy & Constitution event.

Paul Revere House

Rhett led his group down the streets of Boston at a fast pace. They started at The Paul Revere House, where instead of

going inside, Rhett quickly snapped a photo and moved on. What he missed in the moment was finding out that the Paul Revere House is actually the oldest building in downtown, and one of the few Revolutionary Era buildings still standing! After Paul Revere sold it, it was used for various commercial purposes. In 1902, Paul Revere's great-grandson, John P. Reynolds Jr. purchased the building to ensure that it would not be demolished. Over the next few years, the Paul Revere Memorial Association was created and money was raised to renovate the building. Once the renovations were complete, it was officially opened to the public in order to showcase its former owner's story.

Paul Revere Monument

While Rick and Kamryn were still driving, Rhett's crew kept making their way to locations. Although Rhett might have gotten them lost a couple of times along the way... They finally found the Paul Revere Monument, sculpted by Cyrus Edwin Dallin.

The Mechanics

Rhett's group also found a plaque close to the monument that details the "Mechanics," America's first intelligence gathering network. This group of thirty men (according to Revere's writings) would take turns in pairs patrolling the streets at night in order to gather intelligence on the British troops movements. They would also sabotage and steal British equipment in Boston.

Sybil's Midnight Ride

While Rhett was learning about the Mechanics, Kamryn and Rick had arrived at Carmel, New York, to learn about Sybil from an expert. Vincent Dacquino explained that Sybil had accomplished far more than just one night of riding. She had grown up around greatness, with her father (A Colonel in the local militia) being actively involved in the  events of that era. Vincent also explained Sybil's situation so that we clearly understood what incredible challenges she overcame. The British had burned Danbury, Connecticut, 25 miles away from where Sybil's father was stationed. He needed to organize his men, but they were spread out over a large area and he had no one to retrieve them. Sybil volunteered, and that night she rode 40 miles to warn all 400 of her father's men to muster up, prepare to fight the British, and march to where her father was waiting. She rode through the rain, mud, and dangerous back trails. She not only warned all of her father's

men in the surrounding area, but she made it back to her father's home so that she could be ready to continue helping him if needed! As Vincent explained, at only sixteen years old, she rode three times as far as Revere in far worse conditions and unlike Revere, she did not get caught!

Old North Church

While Kamryn and Rick finished up their interview with Vincent, Rhett's crew came to the church where Revere's men hung the famous lanterns, warning of the British arrival. Although they were only up for a minute  or two, that was plenty of time for the militia of Charleston to see the lights and prepare themselves.

Sharing Our Findings

What started out as a competition turned into a terrific group effort as Kamryn and Rhett joined Dad on stage to present their research.

EPISODE 10

Rhett's Final Thoughts:

I guess I started off rooting for Paul Revere to be the best rider, but it turns out Sybil did some really amazing things as well. I also learned that while great sacrifice is needed in times of war, there are still plenty of ways for us to sacrifice and serve others in ordinary ways. You and I may not be able to ride and rope like the Pattersons or the Midnight Riders, but there are plenty of ways we can help and serve those around us. I also found out that "research" with Brad is fun even when he wins most of the games at Laser Craze!

— Rhett

Discussion Questions

1. How old was Sybil Ludington when she made her ride?

2. How many men did Sybil gather for her father?

3. What organization was Paul Revere a part of that gathered intelligence?

Essay Questions

1. Sybil Ludington volunteered to do a tough job, one that was outside of what others like her would be asked to do. Why is it important for us to be willing to do whatever is necessary, even when it's a hard job?

2. In your opinion, who was the more impressive rider, Paul Revere or Sybil Ludington?

Guest Profile:
The Patterson Family
Boss Your Heart Ministries: In Memory of
Christyn Joy Patterson

In 2009 the Patterson Family adopted their precious little 4 year old, Chrissie, from Serbia. Chrissie celebrated her fourth birthday in the arms of her new forever mommy and daddy. Chrissie was born with several congenital heart defects. She was registered for international adoption when she turned 3, then a total of four different families committed to adopting her, only to back out when they found out more about her medical needs. God called the Patterson family to adopt Chrissie, and when they asked God why all of the other families backed out, He said, "Because she is yours." The Pattersons joyfully obeyed His call, and Chrissie was able to spend 6 loving months with them at their ranch in Texas and another

month fighting for her life after open-heart surgery. Chrissie was full of joy with an infectious smile and contagious laugh. During her six months with the Pattersons, she was loved and cherished. She was the  life of the party everywhere she went, and she loved being their "princess".

Boss Your Heart Orphan Ministries was created as a way of carrying out Chrissie's legacy, helping orphans around the world in memory of Chrissie.

The Pattersons have adopted 10 children, most of them with special needs. Please consider supporting Boss Your Heart Ministries with a tax-deductible donation at www.bossyourheart.org.

Passing the Torch of Freedom

Our busiest, and also most inspiring time of the year happens each summer when we travel from Capitol to Capitol across America training young leaders during Patriot Academy. This year was extra special because it was Kamryn's first time to join her older brothers in participating as a student-legislator. She was so nervous when it was time to present her bill in committee that I thought she was actually going to pass out... or punch me for pushing her to do it. I wasn't sure which might happen! Thankfully, Trey and Reagan came along and encouraged her and coached her and convinced her to go through with it. Then once she got to the podium and started speaking into the mic, she pushed past the fear and did an amazing job. I was so proud of her! While this episode zeroes in on Kamryn's personal experience, we hope everyone watching will be inspired by the hundreds of young people you will see passionately articulating the principles upon which the nation was built and showing the way to restore them.

- Rick

EPISODE 11

Patriot Academy

Founded in 2003 by Rick and Kara (with huge help from David & Cheryl Barton!), Patriot Academy has become the premier leadership academy in the nation for students who desire to find their life purpose,

discover the political process, and learn leadership skills that will help them in all walks of life. Patriot Academy has grown and expanded to state capitols across the nation and hundreds of students graduate from the program each and every year. These students go on to become politically active, start businesses, make movies, practice law, pursue the missionary field, and pursue many other areas of life. One of the beautiful things about Patriot Academy is that the skills learned by the students can be applied to all areas of life. We believe that Christians should be salt and light in all areas of the culture, and that we should not hide the gospel or truth from any area of our society.

Patriot Academy gives students between the ages of 16-25 the chance to be around like-minded individuals, who are passionate and desire to make a difference in the world around them. Throughout the week, the students participate in an extremely realistic simulated legislative session, while also participating in courses designed to help them find what they are here on earth to do, and what area of the culture they can help effectively change for good. They are trained by Rick and other communication experts in everything from how to gain rapport with someone in a business meeting to how to conquer their fear of public speaking. Former and current legislators help coach them on public policy, philosophy, and

theology while helping the students discover and put into practice the Timeless Principles of Liberty. Most importantly, the students are taught the importance of character, morals, and integrity.

Kamryn's Journey during Patriot Academy

Our entire family looks forward to Patriot Academy each and every year. It is a chance for each of us to grow, work on

EPISODE 11

our skills, and serve other students throughout the week. This year at Patriot Academy was interesting, as Kamryn was finally able to join Trey and Reagan as a student in the program. Every student at Patriot Academy has to bring a piece of legislation that they write themselves. She was nervous, but she fought through it like

a champ (thanks to a lot of family encouragement!) and successfully passed her bill out of committee! She fearlessly jumped into the process and made the family proud.

Ceremonial Passing of the Torch

The Banquet at the end of Patriot Academy is a powerful experience for students, parents, and guests. After spending a week going through intense leadership training, the

WWII MARINE BILL JOHNSON

students get the chance to receive a personal charge from American war veterans. While they physically pass the torch o freedom to the students in the form of a medal, these veteran look the students in the eye

General Sam Turk

and charge them with the task of protecting freedom on their watch. The entire process is extremely moving, with very few dry eyes by the end of the evening.

This particular year, our guest speaker was WWII Marine Edgar Harrell. As a survivor of the sinking of the USS Indianapolis by a Japanese submarine, Edgar Harrell was able to remind the students of the sacrifice given by previous generations. He then charged the students with making sure to live out their freedom and never let it go to waste.

WWII MARINE EDGAR HARRELL
SURVIVOR OF U.S.S. INDIANAPOLIS AND AUTHOR

Torch of Freedom

Edgar Harrell's words perfectly set up our ceremony at the end of Patriot Academy. In order to visually paint a picture of how quickly freedom and liberty can spread, we have a ceremony where the

SGT. JOHNATHAN REYNA
COMBAT VETERAN OF OPERATION IRAQI FREEDOM

students actually light their torch, take it throughout the crowd, and spread it to each group. It helps show the students that they are now equipped and trained to go into the real world and spread freedom across their community.

The Torch of Freedom represents the Timeless Principles of Liberty that work every time they are applied. It represents freedom and liberty even in the face of tyranny. It represents the sacrifices of good men and women so that future generations can be free to live their lives in peace and safety. It is not a self-sustaining flame. It must be stoked and guarded, purposefully and intentionally passed from generation to generation. It must be shielded when evil tries to snuff it out and it must be stoked when the people forget what it takes to have these Blessings of Liberty.

The question is, will there be enough Patriots left to keep

the flame alive? There has always been a remnant of heroes willing to sacrifice their lives, fortunes, and sacred honor to protect the Torch of Freedom. They did not always get credit or recognition, but they always stepped up to the plate when *duty called*.

The Torch of Freedom is under attack daily in our modern society. Freedom and responsibility is constantly being thrust to the side in favor of entitlement and control. ***Where will you be when the Torch of Freedom is under attack?*** When darkness and evil are trying their best to put the flame out, how will you respond? It is our hope and prayer that you will join us in the fight to protect freedom. That you will join us; we few, we happy warriors, we Patriots.

EPISODE 11

Rick's Final Thoughts:

Edgar Harrell's speech was such an amazing inspiration to the Green family and to all the Patriot Academy students and parents. I had the privilege of interviewing Mr. Harrell for WallBuilders Live!, the daily radio show David Barton and I do. Mr. Harrell was already in his 90's at the time of the interview, yet so passionate and articulate that I had to ask, "Do you ever do speaking engagements?" Mr. Harrell said, "About 30 a year, send me an email and we'll see what we can do!" Three months later, Mr. Harrell was with us at Patriot Academy. You can get his inspiring true story through his book, Out of the Depths.

— Rick

Special Mention:
USS Indianapolis

The world's first operational atomic bomb was delivered by the Indianapolis, to the island of Tinian on 26 July 1945. The Indianapolis then reported to CINCPAC (Commander-In-Chief, Pacific) Headquarters at Guam for further orders. She was directed to join the battleship USS Idaho at Leyte Gulf in the Philippines to prepare for the invasion of Japan. The Indianapolis, unescorted, departed Guam on a course of 262 degrees making about 17 knots.

At 14 minutes past midnight, on 30 July 1945, midway between Guam and Leyte Gulf, she was hit by two torpedoes out of six fired by the I-58, a Japanese submarine. The first blew away the bow, the second struck near midship on the starboard side adjacent to a fuel tank and a powder magazine. The resulting explosion split the ship to the keel, knocking out all electric power. Within minutes she went down rapidly by the bow, rolling to starboard.

Of the 1,196 aboard, about 900 made it into the water in the twelve minutes before she sank. Few life rafts were released. Most survivors wore the standard kapok life jacket. Shark attacks began with sunrise of the first day and continued until the men were physically removed from the water, almost five days later.

EPISODE 11

Of the 900 who made it into the water, only 317 remained alive. After almost five days of constant shark attacks, starvation, terrible thirst, suffering from exposure and their wounds, the men of the Indianapolis were at last rescued from the sea.

"The Story". www.ussindianapolis.org. Retrieved from http://www.ussindianapolis.org/story.htm.

Essay Questions

1. Why is it important that we honor the generations that have come before us?

2. Why is it important that we be willing to accept the Torch of Freedom, and all the responsibilities that come with it?

3. What can you do today to help protect the Torch of Freedom?

Season Finale

In our season finale, you'll notice that this episode is slightly different than most of the others. We are not tackling a myth, although there is some investigating that occurs. This episode is much more about going on a journey. We begin with some work on our ranch in Dripping Springs, Texas. My best friend and first love, Alexandra Murphy, had recently come down from Delaware to attend Patriot Academy, and was helping us get ready to host a 'regional' Patriot Academy in the Northeast. She was also helping us write a book called Legends of Liberty, when some problems arose that put our schedule into hyperdrive, overdrive, and warp speed... all at once! Eventually, we were able to find a solution and finish the book just in time, as well as accomplish a few other momentous things during our trip to the northeast. In the end, it was a great trip with a lot of great memories made. I hope you enjoy this episode as you come with us on this fun journey, all while being entertained by Rhett's hilarious (and misguided) attempts to discover my plans throughout the episode.

- Trey

The Question:

What is next for the Green family? Will this season end with a big finale or a clifhanger...?

EPISODE 12

EPISODE 12

Construction Project!

We start off this trip in the middle of a construction project at home on our ranch. Projects like this are not uncommon,

but this one had a special purpose. While we all worked to clear off a piece of land and set the foundation for a concrete slab, Rhett spent all of his time trying to figure out what we were building.

In the middle of clearing off some brush, we got a call from our good friend Gary Newell. As one of the contributing authors to the new book, Gary was excited to share the good news that we had been invited to launch the book at a major speaking engagement with over 10,000 people! The family was excited, but we

also knew that we were a long way from finishing the book, *Legends of Liberty*, and this call just ramped up our deadline by a couple of months.

Legends of Liberty

Legends of Liberty is a recounting of fifteen incredible Legends throughout history. Written by twelve different authors and compiled by Rick, *Legends of Liberty* investigates what it was about these particular Legends that made them so successful, and then explains how we can apply those principles in today's world. Although it took some rushing to get it ready in time for our events, it rolled off the presses power packed with amazing stories. The contributing authors are David Barton, Cliff Graham, Rick Green, Gary Newell, Brad Stine, Krish Dhanam, Kamryn Green, Tim Barton, Reagan Green, Paul Tsika, Alexandra Murphy, and Trey Green.

Some of the Legends covered in the book are well known, while others are unsung heroes. They are John Locke, King David, Nathan Hale, Squanto, Jackie Robinson, Zig Ziglar, Sybil Ludington, George Washington, Brian Birdwell, Jimmy Robertson, Dicey Langston, Moe Berg, Wentworth Cheswell, Peter Francisco, and Sujo John.

EPISODE 12

Each of these Legends has something in their story that we can learn and apply to our daily lives. The twelve authors take those principles and illustrate how they can be applied in today's society, and the impact those principles can have on the world around us.

Task Manager

While we all worked on our parts of the book and got packed, Mom kept everyone on task. She kept up with all  the little things that needed to be done, from chapter revisions for the book to packing up all of our Patriot Academy materials.

Love in the Air!

After Trey finished helping Kara, he joined Alexandra outside to help with writing her Betsy Ross chapter of the book. Trey and Alexandra met through family connections and Patriot Academy. They are each other's first and only love, which has made for a very special relationship. Beginning as friends, their relationship grew to be each other's closest confidant over the course of two years.

Although Alexandra still lived in Delaware at this time, she often traveled with the family to events and Patriot Academies to help out wherever needed. Meanwhile...

Kamryn On Sybil

...Kamryn was working hard on her Sybil Ludington chapter. She had all the right information, but was working overtime to make sure that it flowed smoothly as a short story. Kamryn wrote her Sybil chapter in the "faction" style, which is a combination of accurate non-fiction, with a fiction/novel writing style. She was passionate about getting the story as accurate as possible while still keeping the reader's attention. She was hard at work!

Brad Stine & Jackie Robinson

While Kamryn worked on her chapter, Reagan and Rhett

EPISODE 12

called up Brad to make sure that he hadn't gotten distracted and forgotten any edits to his chapter. Brad ended up not only having his chapter written, but had his final draft edited and finished before the rest of us! Having been a baseball player himself, Brad really enjoyed telling the story of Jackie Robinson.

Betsy Ross

While the others were finishing their chapters, Trey and Alexandra ran into some trouble finding reliable sources on Betsy Ross. While there were rumorsthatshedesignedthe

American flag, they could not find any conclusive evidence to confirm the story. Because no original sources existed, Trey and Alexandra took the issue to Rick, who decided to play it safe and scrap the Betsy Ross chapter.

Betsy, We Have a Problem!

Since we had to scrap the Betsy Ross story, we found ourselves in a predicament. We needed a new opening chapter and we needed it fast! Not only did we need one, but it needed to be good...we wanted it to be really powerful. Rick called a family meeting together in order to discuss a replacement. The family tossed around some ideas, finally deciding on a story that was inspiring and powerful and patriotic...

Nathan Hale

...that story was the life of Nathan Hale! We had told the story of Nathan Hale previously through our speeches on stage, but had never written it into a book. In order to do so, we knew that we needed to research heavily and find the original source of his famous line. Nathan Hale graduated top of his class at Yale and went straight into being a school teacher, with hopes of becoming a minister. As a Captain in Washington's military, he volunteered for an espionage mission that he knew could cost him his life. Although he successfully gathered the necessary information, he was captured on his way back to safety, he was tried, and sentenced to hang the very next morning. Before his hanging, he uttered those now famous words, "I only regret that I have but one life to give for my country."

During Patriot Academy at the Delaware State Capitol, Trey and Alexandra spent their time focused on finding these resources to confirm Hale's story. Digging through academic journals, papers, and books, they finally found some original sources that confirmed the legend of Nathan Hale. Success! Trey and Alexandra were ecstatic, as this meant that they most definitely had their opening chapter.

Nathan Hale was an American officer during the Revolutionary War. He volunteered for a spy mission requested by General Washington.

Meanwhile... Rhett spies on Trey...

While Trey finished gathering a few details for the Nathan Hale chapter, Rhett followed him, believing that he was up to some sort of political maneuvering. Rhett thought he was being sneaky, but he never quite got the information he wanted...

His sleuthing came to an end as everyone got into the bus and made their way to Independence Hall in Philadelphia for a special night (in more ways than one!).

Independence Hall

We had all been to Independence Hall before, but we still get awe struck every time we get the chance to walk these hallowed steps. For this trip, we had a special night for the students of Patriot Academy. We actually held a simulated legislative session on the floor of Congress Hall! The students got up and debated their own bills in the very room where Washington and Adams were both inaugurated and the ratification of the Bill of Rights occurred. The students even had the opportunity to

come forward and add their names to the the Declaration of Independence just like the Founding Fathers.

During the simulated legislative session, students were given the opportunity to pass resolutions in addition to debate bills. This process is actually done in the real Congress and all

state legislatures and the difference is that resolutions will typically be passed to honor someone, or for the state to take an official stand on an issue without actually passing a law. For this particular night, Trey had a very special resolution that he had prepared to present to a special person in attendance in Congress Hall on this trip...

The Proposal

I had no idea that when I entered Independence Hall that night, that I'd leave an engaged woman. I can't say Trey caught me entirely by surprise, but regardless of whether or not I expected the proposal, it became one of the

most treasured memories of my life. Before he got up to pop the question, I had been asked to deliver a resolution thanking the park rangers for their service. I thought it was odd of them to ask me, since I hadn't even written the resolution, but turns out it was all part of the "secret plan" to get the mic hooked up to me, so that the cameramen could pick up "the reaction" for

the show (sneaky, sneaky). I had suspected that Trey might try to propose to me during or after my resolution, but once I delivered the speech and sat down, I was

convinced that Trey wasn't going to propose to me that day. Trey then proceeded to stand and deliver a resolution of his own. At the end of it, like in a dream, he got on one knee and asked me to be his wife. I will never, ever forget that moment, when all I could stutter out was a relieved "Yes" as he slipped a ring over my finger. That was the night we began the next chapter in our lives, and just three months later we became husband and wife. Independence Hall is known for many things, but for me...it'll always and forever more be known as the place where Trey Green finally asked me to spend our lives together, to lock our shields, fight for freedom, and the pursuit of absolute truth. He also asked me to help in bringing up the next generation~ Teehee (Baby Patriots), through the pursuit of a Godly marriage. And of course my answer had to be "Yes. A thousand times yes."

— Alexandra Green

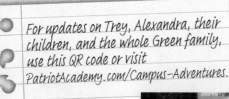

For updates on Trey, Alexandra, their children, and the whole Green family, use this QR code or visit PatriotAcademy.com/Campus-Adventures.

CAMPUS
Adventures

Watch Now ▶

ENDNOTES & BIBLIOGRAPHY

EPISODE 1

Bibliography:

Anderson, Fred. *Crucible of War: The Seven Years' War and the Fate of Empire in British North America, 1754-1766*. Random House, Inc: New York, New York. 2000.

Barton, David. *The Bulletproof George Washington*. Wallbuilder Press: Aledo, TX. 2009.

Chernow, Ron. *Washington: A Life*. The Penguin Press: New York, New York. 2010.

Washington, George. *Letter from George Washington to John Augustine Washington*. July 18, 1755. Located at http://www.loc.gov/teachers/classroommaterials/connections/george-washington/langarts.html. Retrieved on August 26th, 2016.

EPISODE 2

Bibliography:

Christ Church Philadelphia. "Historic Christ Church". *www.christchurchphila.org*. Last modified, 2007. Accessed on August 27th, 2016. Accessed from http://www.christchurchphila.org/Historic-Christ-Church/73/.

Christ Church Philadelphia. "The Graves". *www.christchurchphila.org*. Last modified, 2007. Accessed

on August 27th, 2016. Accessed from http://www.christchurchphila.org/Historic-Christ-Church/Burial-Ground/The-Graves/98/.

Park Ranger EDU. "What is a Park Ranger"? *www.parkrangeredu.org*. Last modified, 2016. Accessed on August 27th, 2016. Accessed from http://www.parkrangeredu.org/what-is-a-park-ranger/.

Platt, John D. R. *Historic Structure Report: Graff House: Historical Data Section*. Independence National Historical Park: Philadelphia, Pennsylvania. 1972. https://www.nps.gov/parkhistory/online_books/inde/graff_house_hsr.pdf.

National Park Service. "Declaration House". *www.nps.gov*. Accessed on August 27th, 2016. Accessed from https://www.nps.gov/inde/learn/historyculture/places-declarationhouse.html.

National Park Service. "Independence Hall". *www.nps.gov*. Accessed on August 27th, 2016. Accessed from https://www.nps.gov/inde/learn/historyculture/places-independencehall.html.

National Park Service. "Congress Hall". *www.nps.gov*. Accessed on August 27th, 2016. Accessed from https://www.nps.gov/inde/learn/historyculture/places-congresshall.html.

ENDNOTES & BIBLIOGRAPHY

EPISODE 3

Bibliography:

Birmingham Civil Rights Institute. "About BCRI". *www.bcri. org*. Accessed on August 29th, 2016. Accessed from http:// www.bcri.org/Information/AboutBCRI.html.

Fairclough, Adam. "Was Martin Luther King a Marxist?" *History Workshop*, no. 15 (1983): 117-25. http://www.jstor. org/stable/4288462.

Marx, Karl. "A Contribution to the Critique of Hegel's Philosophy of Right". *www.marxists.org*. Accessed on August 30th, 2016. Accessed from https://www.marxists.org/ archive/marx/works/1843/critique-hpr/intro.htm.

Marx, Karl & Engels, Frederick. *The Communist Manifesto: A Modern Edition*. Verso: New York, New York. 1998.

National Park Service. "Ebenezer Baptist Church". *www.nps. gov*. Accessed on August 29th, 2016. Accessed from https:// www.nps.gov/malu/planyourvisit/ebenezer_baptist_church. htm.

EPISODE 4

Bibliography:

Arlington Cemetery. "Brochure". *www.arlingtoncemetery. com*. Accessed on August 30th, 2016. Accessed from http://www.arlingtoncemetery.mil/Portals/0/Web%20Final%20PDF%20of%20Brochure%20March%202015.pdf.

Arlington Cemetery. "President John Fitzgerald Kennedy Gravesite". *www.arlingtoncemetery.mil*. Accessed on August 30th, 2016. Accessed from http://www.arlingtoncemetery.mil/Explore/Monuments-and-Memorials/President-John-F-Kennedy-Gravesite.

Audie Murphy Memorial Website. "Photos". *www.audiemurphy.com*. Accessed on August 30th, 2016. Accessed from http://www.audiemurphy.com/photo_por_160.htm.

Audie Murphy Memorial Website. "Biography". *www.audiemurphy.com*. Accessed on August 30th, 2016. Accessed from http://www.audiemurphy.com/biography.htm.

Audie Murphy Memorial Website. "Decorations". *www.audiemurphy.com*. Accessed on August 30th, 2016. Accessed from http://www.audiemurphy.com/decorations.htm.

ENDNOTES & BIBLIOGRAPHY

National Park Service. "History of the Marine Corps War Memorial". *www.nps.gov*. Accessed on August 30th, 2016. Accessed from https://www.nps.gov/gwmp/learn/historyculture/usmcwarmemorial.htm.

Tomb Guard. "Tomb Guard". *www.tombguard.com*. Accessed on August 30th, 2016. Accessed from https://tombguard.org/tomb-of-the-unknown-soldier/the-tomb-guard/.

EPISODE 5

Bibliography:

Strand, Kenneth A. "Some Significant Americana: The Saur German Bibles". *Andrews University Studies*. Vol. 32, Nos. 1-2, 57-106. (1994). Accessed from https://www.andrews.edu/library/car/cardigital/Periodicals/AUSS/1994-1/1994-1-06.pdf.

WallBuilders. "Overview". *www.wallbuilders.com*. Accessed on September 1st, 2016. Accessed from http://wallbuilders.com/ABTOverview.asp.

John Marshall Foundation. "Life and Legacy". *www.johnmarshallfoundation.org*. Accessed on September 1st. Accessed from http://www.johnmarshallfoundation.org/john-marshall/life-legacy/.

Biographical Directory of the United States Congress. "Ellery, William, (1727 – 1820). *www.bioguide.congress.gov*. Accessed on September 1st. Accessed from http://bioguide.congress.gov/scripts/biodisplay.pl?index=E000115.

Tolle Lege Press. "Discover the New 1599 Geneva Bible".

www.genevabible.com. Accessed on September 1st, 2016. Accessed from http://www.genevabible.com/genevaHome.php.

EPISODE 6

Bibliography:

The Lexington Historical Society. "Historic Structure Report: The Hancock-Clarke House." *www.lexingtonhistory.org*. Accessed on September 2nd, 2016. Accessed from http://www.lexingtonhistory.org/uploads/6/5/2/1/6521332/hsr_full.pdf.

The Lexington Historical Society. *First Shot: The Lexington Revolutionary Experience*. Ambit Press. 2011.

The Library of Congress. "Today in History: July 13th."

www.memory.loc.gov. Accessed on September 1st, 2016. Accessed from https://memory.loc.gov/ammem/today/jul13.html.

ENDNOTES & BIBLIOGRAPHY

Crowell, Preston. "*Stow, Massachusetts: 1683 - 1933.*" Preston R. Crowell: Stow, Massachusetts. 1933.

National Park Service. "Lexington and Concord: A Legacy of Conflict." *www.nps.gov*. Accessed on September 2nd, 2016. Accessed from https://www.nps.gov/mima/learn/education/upload/Minute%20Man%20Lesson%20Plan.pdf.

EPISODE 7

Bibliography:

Leitch, Alexander. "Davies, Samuel". *www.etc.princeton.edu*. Accessed on September 5th, 2016. Retrieved from https://etcweb.princeton.edu/CampusWWW/Companion/davies_samuel.html.

Historic Polegreen Church Foundation. "The Polegreen Story". *www.historicpolegreen.org*. Accessed on September 5th, 2016. Retrieved from http://www.historicpolegreen.org/story/.

United States Congress. "MUHLENBERG, John Peter Gabriel, (1746 - 1807). *www.bioguide.congress.gov*. Accessed on September 6th, 2016. Retrieved from http://bioguide.congress.gov/scripts/biodisplay.pl?index=m001066.

United States Congress. "MUHLENBERG, Frederick Augustus Conrad, (1750 -1801). *www.bioguide.congress.gov.* Accessed on September 6th, 2016. Retrieved from http://bioguide.congress.gov/scripts/biodisplay.pl?index=m001063.

EPISODE 8

Bibliography:

Library of Congress. "Religion and the Founding of the American Republic." *www.loc.gov.* Accessed on September 2nd, 2016. Retrieved from https://www.loc.gov/exhibits/religion/rel04.html.

Freedoms Foundation. "The Bill of Responsibilities." *www.freedomsfoundation.org.* Accessed on September 2nd. Retrieved from http://www.freedomsfoundation.org/billofresponsibilities.

Independence Hall Association. "Carpenters' Hall." *www.carpentershall.org.* Accessed on September 2nd, 2016. Retrieved from http://www.carpentershall.org/index.htm.

Henry Armitt Brown. "Oration – Anniversary of Continental Congress – 1874." *www.wallbuilders.com.* Accessed on September 2nd, 2016. Retrieved from http://www.wallbuilders.com/libissuesarticles.asp?id=158412#R3.

ENDNOTES & BIBLIOGRAPHY

National Park Service. "Washington Crossing State Park."

www.nps.gov. Accessed on September 2nd, 2016. Retrieved from https://www.nps.gov/nr/travel/delaware/was.htm.

McCullough, David. "*1776*." Simon & Schuster:

Barton, David. The Bulletproof George Washington. Wallbuilder Press: Aledo, TX. 2009.

Chernow, Ron. *Washington: A Life*. The Penguin Press: New York, New York. 2010.

EPISODE 9

Bibliography:

Hardin, Stephen L. "*Texian Iliad*". University of Texas Press: Austin, Texas. (1994).

EPISODE 10

Bibliography:

Paul Revere Memorial Association. "Paul Revere's Home." *www.paulreverehouse.org*. Accessed on September 3rd, 2016. Retrieved from https://www.paulreverehouse.org/about/paulreverehouse.html.

Central Intelligence Agency. "Intelligence Throughout History: Paul Revere's Midnight Ride." *www.cia.gov*. Accessed on September 3rd, 2016. Retrieved from https://www.cia.gov/news-information/featured-story-archive/2010-featured-story-archive/intelligence-history-paul-revere.html.

EPISODE 11

Bibliography:

Indy Survivor. "Bios". *www.indysurvivior.com*. Accessed on September 4th, 2016. Retrieved from http://www.indysurvivor.com/categories/126632B1-B267-E9D0-DF65FFCA8F1C2E8D/bios.html.